TICKET TO
Curlew

BY
Celia Barker Lottridge

ILLUSTRATIONS BY
Wendy Wolsak-Frith

A GROUNDWOOD BOOK
Douglas & McIntyre
Vancouver/Toronto

Groundwood Books
Douglas & McIntyre
585 Bloor Street West
Toronto, Ontario M6G 1K5

We acknowledge the support of the Canada Council for the Arts
and the Ontario Arts Council for our publishing program.

Canadian Cataloguing in Publication Data

Lottridge, Celia B. (Celia Barker)
Ticket to Curlew
ISBN 0-88899-221-1
I. Title.
PS8573.088T53 1994   jC813'.54   C94-931121-9
PZ7.L67Ti 1994

Special thanks to the Writer in Residence Program of the
Regina Public Library.

Illustrations by Wendy Wolsak-Frith
Design by Michael Solomon
Printed and bound in Canada

For my father, Roger Garlock Barker,
who told me stories of the prairies,
and his father and mother,
Guy and Cora Barker.

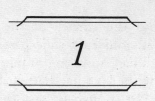

1

THE conductor walked down the swaying aisle of the passenger car. He touched the back of each seat lightly as he moved along, looking up at the ticket stubs in the holders on the luggage rack. When he passed Sam and Pa's seat he called out, "Curlew! Next stop, Curlew, Alberta!"

Sam was on his feet in a second, reaching up for his satchel. He had been sitting in that seat for three days, ever since they had changed trains at Winnipeg.

Sam liked the train. He liked the idea that while he was just sitting there, even sleeping, he was travelling over land he had never seen before. But three days of sitting was enough.

"No need to hurry, son," said Pa. "You know they call the stations a good ten minutes early."

But Sam was in no mood to wait. He lugged his heavy satchel out onto the open platform at the end of the car. He had spent a lot of time out here during the journey. The air blowing across the platform always felt fresh, even when it was mixed with smoke from the engine. Sometimes the sound of the rumbling wheels and the screeching joints of the train was so loud that Sam could shout and no one heard him. If he looked down he could see the rails snaking past and watch the coupling between the cars shift.

He leaned into the corner of the railing and watched the green-gold land slide past. Since early morning the track had run along a range of low treeless hills, but now the land had flattened out again.

Sam sighed. Even though Pa said the flat prairie was best for farming, Sam secretly hoped Curlew would be set on the highest hill in eastern Alberta. But the track ran on as straight and level as if it had been laid out by a giant with a yard stick.

Pa came through the door carrying his satchel and the big wooden toolbox and stood beside Sam. He set the satchel down but kept a firm grip on the toolbox. It was precious. The tools had belonged to Great-grandfather Ferrier, a famous woodworker. Famous in the northwest corner of Iowa, anyway, where he had built dozens of schoolhouses and churches.

Back in Iowa Great grandfather's tools had hung on the wall of the workshop behind the house. Each hammer, bit and file had its proper place. When the Ferriers decided to move to Canada, Pa built a box with a special space for each tool. Some of the biggest saws and the adze wouldn't fit into the box. They were back in the freight car so that Pa and Sam had with them all the tools they needed to build a house for the family. Mama and Josie and Matt would come later in the summer when everything was ready for them. ·

The train slowed, jerked and stopped. There was a hiss of steam, and a bell rang. They had arrived at Curlew.

Sam jumped down from the train before the conductor had time to lower the steps. In front of him was a small station building just like dozens of others they had passed on the journey. Sam was not interested. He wanted to see the town. He set his satchel down beside Pa who was having a last chat with the conductor. Then he walked to the far end of the station platform and looked at Curlew.

He saw one street with small wooden buildings straggling along it. There was a church, not nearly as fine as any Great-grandfather had built. The street was dirt with deep ruts that must have been made in mud time. Along the edges boards had been laid to make a sidewalk just wide enough that two people could pass if they were careful.

At least one of the buildings was a store. *J. T. Pratt, Dry Goods and Groceries* was painted on its high flat front. Beside it was a smaller building with lumber and coal stacked next to it. There was not a single tree anywhere, but some of the doorsteps had blue and yellow flowers blooming beside them.

Pa joined Sam at the edge of the platform. "I guess you can see all there is of Curlew from right here," he said.

"I guess so," said Sam. He couldn't think of another word to say. For some reason he had been sure that Curlew would be different from all the little prairie towns he had seen from the train. Curlew would be more like Jericho, Iowa, where they had started their trip. Jericho had trees and painted houses and wide wooden sidewalks. Curlew looked as if it might disappear any minute, swept away by the prairie wind.

But Pa took a deep breath of that wind and said, "New country. That's what it is, new country. In five years you won't know this town. People are coming from everywhere to this spot."

Pa loved meeting new people and talking to them. It seemed to Sam that he had told everyone on the train about his plans. "My father left a good Iowa farm to my brother and me," Pa would say. "But it just wasn't big enough to support two families. I'm the one with wanderfoot, so I was glad to sell out to my brother and buy some of this newly opened-up land in Alberta. Now we're headed for a new life. How about you?"

Then he would listen to what the other person had to say. Sam had heard a lot of stories on the train. There were other hopeful travellers who had come up from the States, drawn by advertisements for free or cheap land. Many were moving from eastern Canada because their farms were too small or their land was wearing out. Some were just looking for adventure.

None of the people they had swapped stories with had gotten off at Curlew, though.

Pa put his hand on Sam's shoulder. "We'd better stop gawking at the big city, son," he said. "They're unloading the freight car."

Before long Pa and Sam had gathered together all the belongings they had brought with them: the axe, saws and adze, the bundled-up tent and a few boxes of provisions. Everything else would come later with the rest of the family. Pa's farm implements, the furniture, even the cows, horses and chickens would all be loaded into a freight car to travel from Jericho to Curlew. A young man from Jericho who was eager to see the west would ride in the freight car and look after the livestock on the journey.

Now Pa looked at their small pile of belongings and said, "The Canadian Pacific Railway calls our big shipment Settler's Effects. I guess we can call this batch Basic Necessities."

Then he left Sam to stand guard over their Basic Necessities while he inquired at J.T. Pratt's store about the agent he had hired to get them a wagon and two horses and a plough. The plough they had had back in Iowa would not do the job of breaking up the tough roots of the prairie grass for the first time.

The agent turned out to be the brother of J.T. Pratt. "How do you do, Mr. Pratt," said Sam politely when Pa introduced him.

"Don't call me Mr. Pratt," said the young man. "That's what they call my brother. Call me Chalkey." He grinned and pointed to his white-blond hair. "Ask me anything you want to. I might even know the answer."

But it seemed to Sam that Chalkey answered most questions without being asked. As Pa said later, he was a regular fountain of information. He told them all about the rainfall that spring, how promising the crops were looking, and the amazing number of people who were coming out to settle around Curlew.

"We're starting up a school," he said to Sam. "Got to give you young people an education. It'll be close in to town here so you'll have about five miles to travel. Your folks will want you to go, I suppose."

"That's for sure," said Sam, but he wondered how Josie and Matt would manage to walk five miles to school. Josie was barely eight and Matt was six. Ten miles a day would be too much for them. It would even be a lot for him, and he would be twelve before Christmas. But Pa and Mama would think of something. They would never let their children go even a month or two without schooling.

According to Pa, a person with an education could write his own ticket in the world. After all, Pa had an education and he had written a ticket to Curlew.

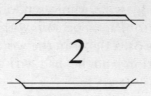

2

By the time all the Ferriers' goods were loaded into the new wagon it was late afternoon, too late to drive out to their land.

"Don't worry," said Chalkey. "We don't have a hotel yet but J.T. and his wife, they'll look after you."

Mrs. J.T., a large woman with jet black hair, welcomed them. "We're always glad to meet new settlers," she said. "It's no trouble at all. We've set up cots in the storeroom for folks who get stranded in town. I hope you don't mind the smell of onions." She chuckled. "The last man who slept there swore he'd get a hotel built before winter just to get away from the onions."

"After nights of sitting up on the train, I can assure you that a cot in a storeroom sounds like luxury," said Pa.

As for Sam, he was so glad to lie down and stretch out that he hardly noticed the smell of onions and leather boots. He just fell asleep.

In the morning Chalkey came by as Pa and Sam were finishing their pancakes and tea at the Pratts' kitchen table. He took them out and showed them the team he'd gotten for them to use until their own horses came up with the Settler's Effects. Pete was a black horse with a white blaze on his forehead, and Goldie's colour matched her name.

"They're strong," said Chalkey, "and used to prairie winters. And they are for sale if you decide you want to buy them later." He walked over to where his own horse was tied. "I'll ride along with you and show you the boundary markers of your land. It can be a little tricky finding them even when you know where to look."

This wouldn't be the first time Pa had seen their piece of land. He had come up two years before, in 1913, when he heard there was good land for sale in the Canadian west. "It's the answer to our problems," he had said when he had returned to Iowa with the deed to two quarter sections of Alberta land in his pocket. "Edward can have this farm and we'll start over. A new start in a new land." His eyes had gleamed at the idea.

Mama had not been quite so sure. "It's a risk, James," she had said, "and a lot of hard work. We don't know the land or the weather out there. But I'm willing to try it."

It had taken two years to arrange everything. Now Mama was packing, Uncle Edward was getting ready to move his family into the old Iowa farmhouse, and Sam was about to get his first look at his new home.

It didn't take long to get out of Curlew. Sam sat beside Pa on the wagon seat and looked around. It was new country, all right, he decided. There were certainly no signs of settlers: no houses, no trees, not even a ploughed field. Of course, the old farm in Iowa had miles of open fields, too. But there were elms around the house and a grove of walnut trees. Sam remembered Mama saying that Great-grandfather had planted all those trees. Maybe that land had been just as empty once.

The sun was hot on the back of Sam's neck, and the dry wind blew his hair into his eyes. Some shade would feel fine right now, he thought. So would some cool water. In Iowa there was the creek where shallow water slid over pebbles all through the summer. The creek had carved out a little valley in the black earth. It was a sheltered, private place. Sam and his cousin Zach liked to sit with their bare feet in the water on a hot day and talk.

Sam looked out over the endless rippling prairie grass. Maybe he could find such a place out there somewhere. But it didn't seem likely.

For a long time they rode in silence. Chalkey, on his big brown horse, led the way along a faint trail in the grass. After a while he dropped back and rode beside the wagon.

"This trail runs along the section line that marks the boundary of your land," he said. "Someday it will be a road. I guess you'll want to build your house somewhere near it." He reined in his horse. "Look, there's one of your markers." He pointed at a small rectangular stone half buried in the grass.

Pa said, "Whoa," to the team. He pushed back his hat and sat with the reins slack, looking past the marker toward the horizon. "Well, Sam," he said, "this is home and you can't beat the view. Why don't you take a look around? Find a good place to build a house."

To Sam the place where they had stopped looked exactly like the rest of the prairie. But Chalkey and Pa knew it was the Ferriers' land. There was no use just sitting in the wagon, so Sam jumped down and began to walk north. He knew it was north because Chalkey had pointed out that all the tracks that would become roads were laid out by the compass. All morning they had been driving west with the sun on their backs.

But if you were away from the track, Sam didn't see how you would know one direction from another. Except for the sun, of course. Even out on this land with no landmarks, the sun would travel from east to west. That was a comfort.

Sam walked as straight north as he could for about ten minutes. Then he stopped and turned around slowly.

He was in the middle of an enormous circle. The horizon might be ten miles away or a hundred. There was nothing — not a tree, not a building, not a fence post — to give him a guide to how far his eyes were seeing. Only grass, ruffled by the wind.

It was a relief to turn his eyes to the south where the wagon, the two men and the horses looked comfortingly solid and perpendicular. A relief from the flatness all around.

Sam ran back to join them just in time to say goodbye to Chalkey who was mounting his horse, getting ready to ride back to Curlew.

"I expect I'll come into town tomorrow, after we see what we're missing out here. We'll need to get a well dug first thing," said Pa. "I'll look you up, anyway."

Chalkey waved and went off, his horse trotting briskly as if it was glad to be going back to a more sociable place.

Pa didn't look after him. Instead he looked out across the expanse of land and nodded in a pleased way. Sam guessed he was seeing a house and a barn and ploughed fields.

After a moment Pa turned back toward the wagon and said, "Now, son, we have work to do. First we should pitch the tent and organize our supplies."

The tent they had brought was just big enough for them to lay out the two bedrolls Mama had made. Their clothes stayed in the satchels.

Pa made a lean-to shelter out of a piece of canvas and two extra tent poles. There they set up their little tin cook stove. They had brought a sack of coal to burn in it since there was no wood to be had out here. The iron skillet, the biscuit tin and their tin plates and utensils were stowed in the supply box along with the crocks of sausage, tins of tomatoes and stout bags of flour, beans and dried fruit that Mama had packed. There was enough food to last them the two months until the family came, but nothing extra.

When everything was in place, Pa smiled at Sam and said, "Now that looks like home." But it didn't, not to Sam. The tent and lean-to looked small and lonely under the huge sky. They looked too small for people to live in. Even people as small under that sky as Sam and Pa.

3

WHEN Sam crawled out of the tent the next morning the sky was pink from horizon to horizon. Pa was busy at the little stove, and Sam sat on his heels and watched the pink grow paler and paler as the sun rose. He waited until the sky was a cloudless blue before he splashed some water from the wash bowl onto his face. Pa had already used that water but it wasn't really dirty. They had to be careful with water. Until they had a well, every drop had to be hauled from town.

Breakfast was oatmeal with dried apples cooked in it, and tea with canned milk. There was no chance of fresh milk until the cows arrived.

After they had eaten, Pa said, "I'm going to go into town and get some advice about a well. I'll feel more comfortable when we have water on the place. You had better come with me. You might get lonely out here."

Sam didn't want to go to town. It would just mean waiting around while Pa talked endlessly with strangers. He looked at the rippling grass spreading all around him and tried to think of a good reason to stay.

"I thought I'd take a walk," he said. "I've been cooped up for a long time."

Pa started to shake his head. Sam added quickly, "We're going to live here, Pa. I can't be going with you every time you leave our place."

"That's true," said Pa. "I guess we both have to get used to being here on our own. But don't go far, son. Keep the tent in sight. That way I won't have to spend valuable time looking for you." He grinned and ruffled Sam's hair.

While Pa hitched up the team Sam made himself busy tidying the supplies in the lean-to. He didn't watch Pa drive away but he could hear the empty wagon jouncing over the ruts in the track. He knew if he saw it getting smaller and smaller until it disappeared he would feel too alone. So he went into the tent and wrote a letter to Mama and Josie and Matt. Pa could mail it the next time he went to Curlew.

Sam wanted to say something encouraging. "We're all settled on our place," he wrote. "At least we're settled in the tent. We haven't met any neighbours yet. There's going to be a school so I guess there are some children around, but I haven't seen any." He didn't want to mention that any neighbours must be miles and miles away.

He stopped writing. Maybe by the next time Pa went to town he would have something funny to tell them. It was strange to think of Mama and the others in the white frame house in Iowa. They were probably sorting out things to bring to a house that wasn't even built yet.

Sam put the letter paper back in his satchel. He decided to explore. There must be something on their land that he couldn't see from here. He wasn't sure where their two quarter sections ended to the west, but he knew they extended some distance to the north, so he headed that way.

He didn't need Pa's warning. He found himself turning often to be sure the tent was still in sight. There was no other landmark to guide him, and his steps left no mark on the springy grass. Prairie wool, Chalkey called it. It was dry and matted underneath with light straight grasses rising from the thick base. There were little blue and purple flowers, too.

Studying the prairie wool Sam saw that there were gopher holes everywhere. It wasn't long before a gopher poked its head out and stared at him. "I wonder if you've ever seen a person before," Sam said to it. The gopher ducked back into the earth.

Now Sam saw that there were faint pathways in the grass that must be the trails of other small animals. Probably rabbits. Maybe Pa would let him shoot a rabbit for dinner sometime. Last night they had had sausage and biscuits. Sausage preserved in lard was the only meat they could bring with them. Already Sam could tell he was going to get pretty tired of it.

He figured he had walked about a mile and the tent was just a little bump far behind him when he saw something white gleaming through the grass up ahead. He couldn't imagine what it was. Pure white and smooth. Bigger than a bucket.

Sam walked faster. Was it a stone? Out here a white stone would seem as strange and foreign as a seashell.

But it wasn't a stone. It was a skull. The huge skull of an animal. An animal with horns. Like a bull, but not quite like a bull.

Suddenly Sam knew. It was a buffalo skull.

Pa had told him about the buffalo, how they used to cover the plains in the thousands and how in recent years they had nearly been killed off by hunters for their skins and tongues. He wondered whether this buffalo had been shot or just died. There was nothing left but the skull.

The buffalo skull made Sam feel like an explorer. He had found something no boy in Iowa had ever found. At least he had never heard of such a thing. He wondered how he would ever find it again. There was no way to mark the place where it lay.

Then he had an idea. "I'll take you back with me," he said to the skull. It felt right to talk to it. After all, it had been a living creature once.

The skull was not heavy. It had lain out under the sun for so long that the heaviness was baked out of it. It was awkward to carry, but Sam didn't mind. The skull proved that there was more to the prairie than grass and sky. Besides, it was something to show Pa.

When Sam got back to the tent he took out the letter again. Now he had some news worth telling. "I found something out on the prairie that you have never seen before. I'm saving it for a surprise. Matt, you will love it. Josie, you will hate it. Mama, you will say it's interesting. I miss you but I'm having a pretty good time. Love, Sam."

Pa was back in plenty of time to cook a supper of sausage and biscuits. He was pleased with Sam's discovery. "This old fellow had quite a life out here in the old days," he said, turning the skull over in his hands. "I guess you could say that this land belonged to the buffalo and the Indians back then."

"How long ago was that?" asked Sam.

"Forty, fifty years," said Pa. "But now it's ours."

But, no matter what Pa said, Sam couldn't feel that this land really was theirs. In the long evenings when Pa was busy with his notebook making plans for the house and the fields, Sam would walk on the prairie and think. He thought about thousands and thousands of buffalo and the Indians on their horses. They would fit this big land. He was getting used to the wide sky and the endless prairie wool, but he still felt very small, like a snail making its slow way across an enormous table.

Pa had chosen a spot for the house, just the right distance from the road. He dug a narrow ditch to show the outline of the walls and where the front door would be. When Sam found three more skulls, he added them to his first find, and put two on each side of the doorway-to-be.

"Do you think your mother's going to be pleased to find a pile of bones in her front yard?" said Pa.

"They mark our place," said Sam. "We can move them later."

Maybe Pa, casting his eyes around the empty sweep of their land, understood what he meant. At least he didn't object when Sam added more skulls to the pile. Sometimes in the night Sam woke up and peered through the tent flap. He could see the bones gleaming white in the moonlight. The sight pleased him. "Good old buffalo skulls," he would whisper and go back to sleep.

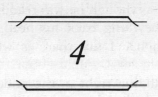

4

ONE morning, before many days had passed, Chalkey drove up in a wagon loaded with metal rods, rough boards and shovels. A grey-haired man as thin and tough-looking as a piece of wire was sitting beside him.

"We've come to find you some water," said Chalkey. "Eli here knows more about water than anyone else in eastern Alberta. He'll tell you where to dig your well."

"I'm pleased to meet you," said Pa. "We don't want to start on the house or the barn until we know where the well is. Tell me, just how do you go about deciding where to dig?"

"Instinct," said Eli. "Backed by scientific method, of course. I have a feel for water and I have a water-testing auger. Mind you, I can't guarantee that we'll find any water at all. It can be mighty scarce out here, Mr. Ferrier."

Sam was worried, and he knew Pa must be, too. They had to have water. But Pa didn't say anything and after a long minute of silence, Eli raised an eyebrow and went on. "Your chances are pretty good, I'd say. I'll just take a walk around."

He paced slowly across the land, starting near the wagon track and zigzagging gradually northward. He walked with his hands clasped behind his back and his head bent, as though he was reading the earth.

Suddenly he flung back his head and raised his right hand high. "I say there is water here!" he exclaimed.

He was standing right in the middle of the very spot where Pa had planned to build the house.

Pa laughed out loud. "Sam," he said, "after all that effort we're going to have to relocate the house."

Sam was so relieved that he laughed, too. Chalkey and Eli stared at them.

"What house?" asked Chalkey, but they were laughing too hard to explain.

"Well, my instinct feels water exactly here," said Eli. "Now we test it." He went over to his wagon and took out some long metal rods. He held one up and said, "It's like a drill, see, and it's hollow at the end. We'll twist it down into the earth at this spot and see whether we bring up anything damp."

"Very ingenious," said Pa, looking closely at the device.

Eli fitted a steel bar crosswise into the top of the auger. Then he and Chalkey and Pa took turns pushing the bar around and around. The auger went down and down into the earth. When the cross bar was about two feet from the ground, Eli pulled it out and fitted another rod into the top of the first one. The cross bar slid into place in the new rod and the drilling went on.

Sam saw that they were drilling into the earth just the way he had many times drilled into a board with one of the drills from Great-grandfather's toolbox.

When they had added another rod and were about ten feet into the ground, Eli drew the whole auger up and shook the dirt out of the hollow end. It was dry.

"We're not anywhere deep enough," he said. "This thing can go twenty-five feet. If we don't get moisture we'll have to try somewhere else. It could take days. But my instinct is strong for this spot."

They added another rod and drilled deeper. There was no way Sam could help, but something kept him watching. As the auger got longer and longer, the turning got harder.

Eli stopped to wipe sweat from his face with a blue bandanna. "At least we haven't hit a rock," he said. "That's one thing that stops this auger cold."

On and on they drilled. Sam was beginning to think that Eli's instinct was wrong. He noticed that they were using the last rod. But this time when they drew up the auger, the earth in the hollow end was damp.

"You'll get a well here," said Eli with satisfaction. "You'll hit water at twenty-two feet."

"This calls for a celebration," said Pa. "Sam and I have been saving some pickles and a jar of peaches for a special occasion. And then we've got a nice soft piece of prairie for you to spread your bedrolls on. Tomorrow we dig."

Sam didn't actually do any digging. There was always a danger that the walls of the well might collapse, even though they were reinforced with boards. Pa built a wheel with a rope and a bucket attached. The man in the hole would load the bucket with earth, and Sam took his turn slowly cranking the filled buckets to the top.

That was hard work in itself. His arms ached after the first day, but the hole was over fifteen feet deep. On the second day Sam figured that each bucket of earth represented about one inch of well. He cranked and thought that he would appreciate water forever after this.

The day went very slowly. About three o'clock Pa was down digging and Sam was cranking, when a small chunk of damp mud flew out of the hole and hit him square in the middle of the forehead.

"Feel that, Sam?" Pa yelled out. "We've got water!"

That night Sam and Pa sat in contented silence eating their biscuit and sausage. Sam thought he could almost hear the well filling with water. He was beginning to believe that they really could live here where the wind always blew and there was nothing to stop the sun. At least they had water.

Pa stretched. "We've done good work, Sam. And now we know just where to put the house and the barn. Tomorrow I'll plough a fire-break around the home place. We don't want to build a house and then lose it in a grass fire."

Sam nodded. He knew that if a broad strip of grass around the buildings was turned under, a prairie fire would turn aside because it had nothing to burn. But he wondered what his next job would be. He could manage Pete and Goldie just fine, but guiding the plough while it cut through the tough sod took more strength than he had.

Pa knew what he was thinking. "There's plenty for you to do, Sam. We need a camp cook, for one thing. You can make our daily bread."

That was biscuit, of course. Pa taught Sam to mix up flour and baking soda and lard with a little water and salt and bake it in the little oven that sat on top of the camp stove.

Sam's first batch of biscuits were chewy. That was a polite way of describing them. "I think you used too much muscle," said Pa. "Biscuits need a light touch. But your next job will need all the muscle you have. You're going to dig us a cellar."

Together they used pegs and string to make the shape of the house on the prairie sod. Then Sam set to digging with a sharp spade that cut through the matted grass roots. In a few days he had made a clear rectangle of bare dirt. Then he began digging down to make a cellar hole. Pa dug, too, once the firebreak was finished.

The cellar would be used for storing food, so it had to be deep enough for Pa to stand up in. That took a lot of digging. When it was finished, Sam couldn't believe how small the hole looked.

"It's supposed to be the beginning of our house," he said to Pa, "but it just doesn't look big enough."

"Don't worry," said Pa. "Everything human-sized looks small out here. Our house will suit us just fine."

But Sam knew the house would be small. All lumber came in by railroad and it was very expensive. Pa planned carefully so that nothing would be wasted. He showed Sam his drawing and paced the rooms off on the sod.

The house would be divided in half lengthwise by a wall. The front half would be the kitchen and sitting-room combined. The back half would be divided into two bedrooms, one for Pa and Mama and one for the boys. Josie would have a bed in the kitchen.

"Josie won't like that," said Sam.

"We'll build her a room as soon as we can," said Pa. "At least she'll be sleeping near the stove."

Sam thought of their house in Iowa. It had a front room and a big kitchen and three bedrooms upstairs. There was a porch to sit on in the summer. He wished for a porch on the new house, but he knew there was no chance. They had to start with the necessities, and a porch was not a necessity. Three rooms with a roof would be sufficient for the family. The next necessity would be a shelter for the animals.

The day Pa went to town to get the lumber, he came back with more than the wagon-load of boards. He had good news.

"We have neighbours to the south," he said. "A man from England and his two grown sons. We've agreed to help each other with house building."

That was good news for sure. Pa could build a house by himself, Sam knew, and he could do a lot to help. But three more men would make the job go fast.

Mr. Martingale and his two sons, Adam and John, arrived the next day in a buggy. They wore tweed trousers and vests and spoke as Sam imagined English gentlemen might speak. They looked strong, though, and they were ready to start building immediately.

"Sam," said Pa, "I want you to take charge of Grandpa's toolbox. You know every tool in it. Make sure we have the ones we need and that they get put back properly."

This job kept Sam busy. He also helped carry boards and hold them in place as the men drove in the nails. He was surprised how fast the house went up.

"A house is just a box, really," he said to himself. The Iowa house had peaked roofs and porches and bits of trim so you didn't notice that it was a box. But this prairie house looked like a box. A small wooden box stuck on that vast flat table of land.

Still, it was solid and it had a good shingle roof. The wooden floor rang with the sound of their boots. The windows—two facing north and two facing south—put frames around the prairie landscape.

Of course, the house was practically empty. Pa and Sam moved their bedrolls and satchels inside, but they still cooked outside on the little tin stove. The kitchen stove and the tin chimney would come with the Settler's Effects. The house waited for the rest of the family and all their things to turn it from a box into a home.

Now Pa and Sam spent three days helping the Martingales build their house just down the wagon track. Sam could see it when he looked out the front windows of the new house. The prairie didn't seem so empty now.

The next big job was to build the Ferriers' barn. Once again Sam helped while Pa and the Martingales built. It was wonderful how much less lonely the house looked with the barn beside it.

Sam moved his buffalo skulls to the south side of the barn where they showed up nicely to anyone riding past. He had nine skulls now. He liked the idea that they were together, a herd of skulls, instead of each one alone.

Sam was becoming an expert skull-finder. He had a system. He asked Pa to bring him a compass from the store in Curlew. Nearly every evening after supper he set out in a new direction. He could use the house as his centre point now. He started by going straight north, the next time north-northwest, then northwest. He could go in a straight line in any direction. No one cared if he crossed their land. Mr. Martingale just said, "If you come across any bodies of water on my land, let me know."

But Sam did not expect to find any bodies of water. How could there be ponds where the land was as flat as a pancake?

He was finding more to see now as he tramped through the prairie wool. Birds' nests and grasshoppers, wild roses and garter snakes. Sometimes by the time he remembered to look back, the house looked so small that he had the feeling it was being pulled away from him. When that happened he always turned around and went back. Even with the compass in his pocket he felt that he might never find the house again if he lost sight of it.

Just when Sam was thinking that he had discovered everything the prairie had to offer, he found something new. He came upon it so suddenly that he nearly fell into it.

It was a hollow in the land, perfectly round and about eight feet across. It looked as though someone had pressed the back of a giant spoon into the earth and turned it round and round.

The sides were smooth and quite steep. Sam ran down the little slope and sat on the ground at the bottom of the hollow. He could see nothing but the rim of grass at the level of his head and the darkening evening sky above him. He felt as if he was in the very centre of the earth.

He stayed there for a long time. He could tell by the light that it was time he headed home, but it was hard to leave that place. Sam noted in his mind that the hollow was directly northwest of the house by his compass. He wanted to be able to find it again.

When he got back to the house, Pa said, "You've been gone a long time. Did you find something interesting?"

"Yes, I did," said Sam, and he told Pa about the little hollow.

Pa nodded. "That must be a buffalo wallow," he said. "I've heard of them. The buffalo liked to roll in the dust. The hollows they wore out with their rolling and turning are called wallows."

"Do you think they came back to them again and again?" asked Sam.

"If it's as big and deep as you say, I suppose they must have."

Sam went out later to look at his buffalo skulls. He tried to imagine the great beasts that could leave dents in the earth with their wallowing. They had made marks on the land that would be there for a long, long time.

He wished he could see the buffalo themselves. On his walks he had seen rabbits and prairie chickens and a lot of gophers but nothing that even came up to his knee. He had never seen the buffalo, but he missed them.

That night Pa and Sam took a few leftover boards and made a rough table. They sat on wooden boxes and ate their supper in the house for the first time.

"We're getting well settled, Sam," said Pa. "We have water and shelter and good neighbours. I'm beginning to feel as if I belong here."

Sam looked around him. The house was empty and bare, but he knew every nail and board. It was his house. When it grew dark he crawled into his bedroll in his own room and fell asleep quickly.

He dreamed that he looked out the window and saw a great brown buffalo standing in the moonlight watching Sam with his small shining eyes. Sam wanted to go out and touch him. But in his dream he knew that the buffalo was only a painting.

Sam opened his eyes. It was dark. The house was around him, and through the window he could see nothing but a million stars.

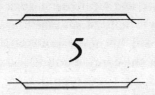

5

IT was nearly high summer. The prairie wool was
beginning to turn brown and thousands of grasshoppers jumped out of the way of the plough as Pa
hurried to get the fields ready for seeding in the
spring. The soil would soon be too dry and hard to
plough, so he worked from early morning until dusk.

Sam was busy, too. He made sure the horses had
feed and bedding in their stalls in the barn. He used
Great-grandfather's files to smooth off the rough
edges of boards in the house, and he drove big nails
into the barn wall and hung up all the tools.

If Pa could spare him, he sometimes went over to
the Martingale place and gave Adam a hand with
fence building. Mr. Martingale and John were
ploughing like Pa, except they had oxen instead of
horses.

"They're the beasts for this country," Mr. Martingale often said. "They're strong and they live on
grass. No oats needed for oxen."

But Pa still liked horses better. "Oxen can't take
the heat," he told Sam. "You have to get up at day-
break and work until dark so they can rest in the
heat of the day. Besides, they're too slow for me.
Walking behind an ox team would put me to sleep."

But Pa got up almost as early as the Martingales.
He made the breakfast porridge before he went out

to the field, but Sam was in charge of the other meals. Supplies were getting very low. He was not sorry that the crocks of sausage were nearly empty. He didn't care if he never saw sausage again in his whole life. But the canned goods and dried fruit were gone. Pretty soon they would have nothing to eat but biscuits and beans.

Luckily Sam's biscuits had improved greatly with practice. It seemed as if he and Pa would never get tired of fresh-baked biscuit.

He remembered the day he and Pa stopped to visit with a young man who was farming a claim about two miles east of their place. He was a bachelor living alone in a tiny shack. "Baching it," Pa called it. It was late afternoon and the man brewed them some tea.

"I'd offer you some biscuit," he said, "but mine's getting mighty stale."

"Don't you bake it fresh every day or two?" asked Pa.

"Bake biscuit?" said the man. "Not me. I came out here to farm, not to bake. My mother baked me up a whole trunkful of dry biscuit back in Ontario. It's lasted me this long but it's running low and getting stale." He shook his head sadly.

On the way home Pa said to Sam, "You're better equipped to take care of yourself than that young fellow is." Sam was pleased. He knew that to Pa, being able to take care of yourself was important. He had just never thought that baking biscuits would be part of it.

"Well, Sam," said Pa one morning not long after this, "in spite of your excellent biscuits I say we've been two bachelors long enough. I think it's time the rest of the family came. What do you think?"

Sam looked closely at Pa. He recognized the twinkle in his eye. "Are they coming soon?" he asked.

"If tomorrow is soon, then they sure are," said Pa.

Sam walked around all day trying to imagine Mama and Josie and Matt in the new house. It was hard. He was used to the quiet and the empty rooms. Tomorrow the house would be full of furniture and boxes—and family! Suddenly Sam could hardly wait.

The next morning Pa had the team hitched up so early that Sam knew he was impatient, too.

"Well, Sam," he said as they drove along the track toward town, "this is the day we've all been waiting for. What do you suppose they're going to think of the new place?"

Sam was surprised. Pa hardly ever seemed to wonder how anyone else would feel about what he had decided to do. He loved new things so much himself.

"I guess they'll think the house is pretty small," he said after awhile.

"But that's just temporary," said Pa. "As soon as we get a good wheat crop we'll build another room or two. It's the land that counts. Your mama knows that. And pretty soon you children will be in school. Then you won't have time to miss the old place."

Just then they passed a little rise in the prairie where three men were nailing beams across the top of a small frame building. Pa waved at them.

"That's the school," he said. "They're hurrying to get it ready by the end of August."

"I thought it would be closer to town," said Sam.

"There are a lot of folks settling to the west of Curlew," said Pa. "It won't be long before the town grows out this far. Anyway, it's better for us. It cuts a mile off the distance you children will have to travel."

"It's still too far for Matt to walk," said Sam. "Even Josie will have a hard time."

"Oh, I've got a plan about that," said Pa. "I just have to talk to Clara." Clara was Mama. She would want to know about the school right away. Before she got married she had been a school teacher herself.

As they drove into town Sam looked around with new eyes. He hadn't been to Curlew since the day they had driven out to their land with Chalkey almost two months ago. Now the street seemed to be bustling with people. Two new stores had gone up. One was a livery stable and the other was a hardware store. Pa looked as proud as if he had built them himself.

"It's a growing town," he said. "I hear there will be a hotel ready for customers before the snow flies."

As they drove up to the station they could see the smoke of the train far off to the east. Pa stopped the team at the edge of the platform. Sam jumped out of the wagon and ran to lean out over the track. He could just see the gleam of the headlight in the distance.

Maybe Matt and Josie were standing on the platform between the cars waiting for their first sight of Curlew. Sam leaned a little farther.

Pa came and laid a hand on his shoulder. "Better step back from the edge, son," he said. "That train will be here before you know it." Sam could tell he was excited, too.

Suddenly Sam heard the chuffing and hissing of the train as the engineer threw on the brakes, and then the loud bell that told everyone in Curlew that the train had arrived. Sam watched the conductor swing down from the train and let down the steps. Matt would come first, he was sure, then Josie, then Mama.

But first came a family with many boys, all wearing wide-brimmed hats, and just as many girls with kerchiefs tied under their chins. Next came several young men laughing and joking with each other.

Then a small boy jumped from the top step.

"Pa!" he yelled. "Sam! We're here!"

The next minute Pa was swinging Matt over his head and giving Josie a big hug. Mama had her hands on Sam's shoulders. She was smiling at him.

"You've surely grown," she said and hugged him.

Sam thought that Matt and Josie were both taller than he remembered, and they looked a little unfamiliar. But Mama was just the same, with her curly brown hair escaping from its bun and her brown eyes smiling and looking a bit anxious at the same time.

Then they all turned and looked at the little station and the dusty main street of Curlew. There was a silence. Sam knew that Josie was comparing Curlew with Jericho, just the way he had.

Before she could open her mouth to speak, he found himself saying quickly, "It's a pretty good town. There's a dry goods store and a livery stable and they're building a school. We saw them this morning." I sound like Pa, he thought. He saw his father grinning at him and he grinned back.

"Yes," said Pa. "Sam and I are settlers now. This is good country. We think you're going to like it, too."

Josie sniffed. Sam knew it was no use telling her what she would like. He reached out and gave one of her braids a tug. He guessed he was glad to see her.

Matt kept asking questions. "Are those our horses? How long will it take to get to our house? Is there a boy my size down the road?" He didn't stop long for answers and he kept running down to the baggage car to see whether their trunk had been unloaded yet.

Mama stood quietly with one hand holding Pa's arm and the other on Sam's shoulder. "I'm glad there's a school and a church," she said, "but I can't wait to see the house. Sam, you're looking so brown. Has your father kept you busy every minute?"

"Without Sam the house and the barn wouldn't have gone up nearly so fast," said Pa. "He's also the best biscuit baker in the territory. I was mighty glad Sam came with me, Clara, especially when I saw how lonesome the bachelors out here get."

There was a long silence. Mama and Pa were both smiling at Sam, and he thought his face must be red. "I'm glad I was here before anything was built," he said at last. "It was something to see, Mama. It really was."

Then Matt came running up and saved him from having to say more. "There's our trunk," he said. "Can we go see our own house now?"

"First we have to collect our livestock and all the rest of our Settler's Effects," said Pa. "It all arrived yesterday. Chalkey is going to help us load up. Sam, you'll be in charge of the cows."

"Me, too!" said Matt. Sam could just see his legs itching to run.

"You, too," said Pa. "Sam will need plenty of help."

It took hours to get everything loaded. Sam was glad to see their own two horses again. Rabbit was a dappled grey horse with extra-long ears and Lady was a patient bay mare. Pa had decided to buy Pete and Goldie, so there would be four horses in their barn. And the two cows and the calf.

Sam and Matt walked along behind the cattle. The beasts were restless from their long journey in the box car. They kept bolting off the track to one side or the other. The boys had to hustle to chase them back. Sam felt good running and shouting with Matt. He had missed his little brother more than he thought.

They were well past the schoolhouse and over halfway home when Sam noticed that the western sky was filling up with dark clouds. Pa saw it, too. He stopped the wagon and came back to say, "We're going to have to hurry, boys. There's a thunderstorm coming up."

The animals seemed to feel the storm coming. They lifted their heads, snorted nervously and trotted faster. The sky was now pale yellow beneath the line of black clouds. The rays of the setting sun cast a slanting golden light that made every blade of grass stand out. Lightning flickered. The wind was blowing more and more fiercely, and it had a cool edge to it.

Sam could see the house now. It seemed that they were racing the storm to see which would get there first. He wondered whether Mama was frightened, but she was sitting up straight on the wagon seat beside Pa with wisps of her hair blowing in all directions. She didn't look frightened at all.

As they all crowded up to the barn, the last brilliant rays of the sun fell on the buffalo skulls. For a moment those empty eyes seemed to be looking at them. Josie moved closer to Pa.

Mama said, "They are interesting, Sam." Matt's eyes opened wide. He was just opening his mouth to ask a question when the sun disappeared and big drops of rain began to fall. The skulls were just a pile of white bones again.

Pa said quickly, "Clara, catch up anything you really need and take Matt and Josie into the house. Sam, you help me unhitch and get the horses into the barn. I'll make sure the canvas on the wagon is secure."

Sam and Pa hurried as much as they could, but by the time the animals were settled, it was nearly dark. Sam followed Pa across the farmyard. Scattered raindrops were still making splotches in the dust, but as Sam stepped through the front door of the house there was a terrific crack of thunder. He shut the door quickly and rain began to pour from the sky onto their new roof.

Pa spread out his arms and said, "Welcome to the prairies."

Mama laughed. "You didn't have to put on such a big show, James. But I promise, this is a homecoming I will never forget."

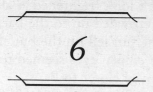

6

PA and Sam spent the next two days putting furniture together and arranging it the way Mama wanted. Most important was the stove. It stood right in the middle of the kitchen where it would be used for cooking and for heat. Nearby under one of the windows was the round walnut table Great-grandfather had made.

"I didn't bring the sideboard," Mama said. "I knew it would be too big for this house. Edward will look after it and someday, when we have space, he'll send it to us."

"I've built plenty of shelves," said Pa. "They'll hold our dishes just fine for now."

Mama's rocking chair and the blue settee filled up the other end of the room. Pa set Josie's bed against the wall. Josie looked at it and set her mouth in a stubborn line.

"I won't sleep there," she said. "At home I had my own room with a windowseat. I won't sleep in the kitchen."

Pa tried to be stern, but Sam could see that he didn't like the look of that bed, either.

"Josie," Pa said, "we all have to do the best we can. You'll have a room of your own when we can buy the lumber. But not now . . ."

"We can rig up a curtain," said Mama. "James, it will just take two posts here near the corners of the bed and Josie will have her own little space. I couldn't bear to leave behind those blue plush curtains from the parlour. Josie shall have them to curtain off her bed."

Pa put up the curtain and, while he was at it, he built three shelves above the bed. Josie unpacked her books and her china cats and the music box Grandma had given her last Christmas. She arranged them carefully on the shelves.

"When I go to bed, everyone will have to go to bed," she told Sam and Matt. "And I will have the only warm bed when winter comes."

For once Sam didn't argue with her snippy remarks. The room he and Matt shared was barely big enough for their two beds. They had hooks on the wall for their clothes and Sam's old wooden toy box for their treasures. That was all, but it was their room and they could shut the door.

In the Settler's Effects had come all the pickles and preserves Mama had put up over the summer. To Sam they made every meal a feast. Matt and Josie couldn't understand why he relished a spoonful of apple butter or a sweet pickle so much. Sam knew the rows of jars on the shelves would barely last till spring. He hoped they wouldn't all end up eating plain biscuits and beans.

Mr. Martingale came over to welcome Mama to the district. "My sons and I are delighted to have you as neighbours," he said. "I confess that I didn't anticipate how far we might be from other settlers. We are fortunate that we live close enough to be of help to each other."

"I was very glad to see a house just across the wagon track," said Mama. "It seems that the prairie can be a lonely place."

"In addition to your arrival I was cheered by the arrival of my books," said Mr. Martingale.

"Books?" said Sam. "Do you have a lot of books?"

"Several crates. I couldn't bear to leave them behind. Most are in Latin, I'm afraid. Remnants of my university days. I don't suppose the Curlew school will be up to Latin for a while, but if you want Shakespeare or translations of the Greek tragedies, you are welcome to borrow what you need."

Sam was a little disappointed. He had hoped for adventure stories or books about birds. But Mama looked pleased that they had such a well-educated neighbour.

"I've heard that a new family has settled about three miles farther west," Mr. Martingale told them. "I believe they have several children."

"We'll have to pay a call," said Mama. "When I've had time to do a baking we'll take them some cinnamon buns."

"Several children," said Josie thoughtfully. "Maybe there's a girl my age who can be my best friend. We can go to school together."

"They are probably boys," said Sam wickedly. "A whole row of boys from Matt's age to mine."

"I don't mind all boys," said Josie haughtily. "Just some I could mention."

Secretly Sam hoped there would be a boy near his age. Now that life was more normal he missed his cousin Zach who had spent a lot of time out on the farm in Iowa. It would be good to start school knowing he already had a friend or at least an acquaintance among the pupils.

Pa, of course, wanted to meet any new neighbours. So a few mornings later when the chores were done they all piled into the wagon. Mama held a pan of buns in her lap.

As they drove west the land seemed to rise a little in long gradual waves. Sam was surprised. When he walked he had the feeling it was perfectly flat. Probably because I'm going so slowly, he thought.

Pa had just said, "We must be getting pretty close," when they all heard a loud barking, and three shaggy black dogs with plumey tails came bounding toward them. In spite of all the noise the dogs seemed friendly as they leaped around the wagon.

"They're saying hello," said Matt, nearly falling out of the wagon as he tried to pat them.

Pa drove slowly on. The dogs raced ahead, barking to announce the arrival of visitors. Then they dashed back as if they were making sure the visitors were really coming. After they had all gone about half a mile this way, three children suddenly appeared. They came running after the dogs, leaping and shouting. Two were small girls, holding up their long skirts as they ran. The biggest was a boy not much older than Matt.

Sam slumped a little. There was no friend for him here. Matt waved at the children and they all waved back.

By now they could see the house. It was small like their own, but it was built of blocks of sod cut right out of the prairie soil. The roof was flat.

"It's a soddy," Pa said. "I've heard of them but this is the first one I've seen."

"Why would anyone build a house out of earth?" asked Josie. "It must be as dark as a hole in the ground."

"You know why," said Mama. "Lumber is costly. Some people spend all they have just to get here. They have to build with what's around them. I do imagine that housekeeping in a soddy is hard work."

Pa stopped the horses and the children stopped, too. They stood in a row staring at the Ferriers with round eyes.

"Hello," said Pa. "We're neighbours and we came by to welcome you to the district. Are your folks at home?"

The three children looked at each other and the boy stepped forward and said something Sam couldn't understand at all. The boy shrugged and smiled. Then he beckoned as if to say, Follow me and started toward the house. The girls and the dogs turned and raced after him.

"I don't know what language that was," said Mama. "I don't think I've ever heard it before."

"You never know who you're going to meet out here," said Pa. "They'll be good neighbours, I'm sure." But Sam could tell he was disappointed that he couldn't swap stories with them.

A man and a woman came out of the sod house and walked toward the wagon. The woman wore a shawl over her hair and the man had a beard, but Sam didn't really look at them. Standing in the doorway was a boy who must be close to his own age. The boy had dark hair and level eyebrows that made him look as if he was frowning a little.

"He's shy," Sam said to himself. "No wonder. A whole wagon-load of us and we don't speak his language." He tried lifting a hand in greeting. After a minute the boy lifted one of his hands. Then he disappeared inside the house.

Pa and Mama were doing their best to talk to the man and woman. They were serious but friendly. They accepted the gift of cinnamon buns with many words that Sam knew were thanks. Mama tried to find out whether the children would be going to school, but the man shook his head and gestured to the land around him.

As they drove home Pa said, "I think he meant that their children will be needed to work on the land. It's too bad. It's the school that will bring all these different people together."

"They have another problem, James," said Mama. "We're four miles from the school. That family must be eight miles. They might as well be forty. We're scattered out here like families of gophers."

"We're not a family of gophers," said Pa. "We're lucky because we can talk to most of our neighbours. We'll find a way to talk to those folks back there, too. As long as we can talk and have a team of horses, there's no reason we can't be as sociable as we want to be."

"Yes," said Josie. "I'm going to go to Sunday School and Mrs. Pratt at the store told me that a piano teacher is coming to Curlew. Can I take lessons?"

"How are you going to get to Sunday School and lessons, Short Legs?" asked Sam. "You won't even walk out to see where I found the buffalo skulls."

"Who cares about old bones," said Josie.

"That's enough," said Pa. "Where there's a will there's a way." He smiled at Josie. "You and I will always find a way to be sociable."

Sam thought again of the boy in the doorway of the soddy. He might be sociable, but no matter what Pa said, if they couldn't talk to each other, how could they get to be friends?

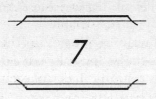

7

MATT was fascinated by Sam's buffalo skulls. He made Sam tell him over and over exactly how he had found them, and every morning at breakfast he said, "Can you take me out to the bone places today, Sam?"

But every day there were jobs to do. Pa had found a stand of buffalo grass and cut it to make bedding for the livestock. Sam spent three days learning to make a proper strawstack. Then there was fence to be strung with wire. Mama needed help, too, getting the house settled.

One day after noon dinner Pa said, "I have to drive in to Curlew to get oats for the horses. Do you boys want to come with me?"

Sam caught Matt's eye. "Matt wants me to take him exploring," he said. "Could we do that instead?" The truth was, Sam missed his long walks. Matt would be good company as well as a good excuse.

"That sounds like a good plan," said Pa.

Mama said, "You had better wait till the worst of the heat is over. Take some bread and jam and water with you. Then you won't have to hurry back for supper. But be back well before dark."

"Oh, we will," said Sam. "It doesn't get dark here till after ten o'clock. Remember, Mama? This is the north."

"Just an Iowa warning," said Mama, and she laughed a little. "But don't be too late."

When they set out, the shadow of the barn was big enough to give the cows some shelter from the hot sun. The boys had only their hats for shade, but there was a light wind and soon the air would start to cool off. Matt was bouncing with excitement.

"You're going to be disappointed," Sam warned him. "There's nothing to find in those places now that I've taken the skulls away. I can't even be sure exactly where they were. I can show you the buffalo wallow, though."

He could tell right away that exploring with Matt was not going to be like exploring alone. Sam had gotten into the habit of keeping to a fairly straight line as he walked across the land. That way it was easy to know what direction to go to head back. But Matt kept seeing interesting things to the right and left—a big tumbleweed, a gopher hole, a bird's nest. Where his attention went, his feet followed.

Sam wasn't worried about getting lost. He knew they were going generally northwest. Anyway, with all Matt's zigzagging and stopping to look, they couldn't get very far.

So he was surprised when he looked back and could see no sign of the house or the barn. They had walked a long way.

Then he turned around and he couldn't see Matt, either.

"Matt," he called sharply. "Where are you? We have to go back."

Matt's voice seemed to come from far away. "Not yet, Sam. Come and see what I've found."

Sam looked in the direction of his brother's voice. There was no Matt to be seen. Sam turned slowly around, trying to make a short brown-haired boy appear. He could see nothing but waving prairie grass clear to the horizon in every direction.

He was alone in the middle of a great round plate that seemed to turn and tilt under him.

"Sam, I'm right over here!" Matt's urgent voice seemed to come from below the earth.

"Where are you, Matt? I can't see you."

"I just went down the hill. Come down, Sam."

"First you come up," said Sam. What was Matt talking about? There were no hills here.

Then, all at once, Matt appeared. He had gotten a good way ahead but he was definitely there.

"Wait, Matt!" Sam yelled, and he began to run toward his brother.

Matt waited. As Sam came up to him he pointed, and Sam saw that he was standing on the edge of a place where the land, instead of being level, sloped sharply down.

"Let's go down," said Matt. He seemed to find the hill perfectly natural, but to Sam it was astounding to be walking down a fairly steep slope in the middle of the prairie.

It wasn't a very long slope. At the bottom was a little grove of trees with dusty silvery-green leaves. The trees weren't much taller than Sam, but their branches drooped toward the ground, making a thick screen. The boys could not see what lay beyond.

Sam looked around. He couldn't see the prairie at all. The slope curved around and blocked out everything but the sky.

Matt began to talk excitedly. "It's a secret place, Sam. No one can see us here." He grabbed Sam's hand and began to pull him into the trees. "It's a jungle," he said. "Maybe there are wild animals. Maybe there are buffalo."

But in twenty steps they were out of the little grove of trees. Or really, Sam saw, they were in a clear space in the middle of the grove. And there they saw not wild animals, but flowers. Red-orange blossoms, a thick carpet of them. They made Sam think of Mama's doorstep garden back in Iowa.

"Look, Matt," he said. "It's not tigers. It's tiger lilies. At least they're spotted like tiger lilies but I think they're even prettier. And no one can see them but us and the birds."

The boys walked all around the edge of the patch of flowers. They were smaller and more red than tiger lilies and they grew so thickly that it would be impossible to walk through them without breaking many of them.

When they had made a complete circle the boys sat under one of the little trees and ate their bread and jam. Mosquitoes sang in the still air, but it was worth some bites to have a real picnic.

Matt said, "Mama won't get to see these flowers and neither will Josie and Papa. We could pick some for them."

"Just a few," said Sam. He was afraid that the flowers they picked would make a hole in the perfect pattern, but when they looked they couldn't see any gaps in the glowing mass of blossoms.

He looked up at the sky. The sun was moving down toward the horizon. There was still plenty of day left, but it was time to be going home.

They went back through the trees and up the slope. When they moved a few steps away from the little valley they couldn't see it at all.

Sam said, "It's hard to believe it's there, isn't it, Matt?"

Matt's eyes shone. "It's a secret," he said. "A real secret."

"It's a secret for sure," said Sam. "I just hope we can find it again." He was hoping even more that they could find their way home. They had wandered around so much that his careful compass reading didn't help.

"If we head straight south," he said to himself, "we'll definitely hit the wagon road. Then we can turn east toward home." He had no idea how far they had come and he could see that Matt was tired. Still, there was nothing to do but start walking.

Matt stayed close to Sam now. That was one good thing. As they plodded along, their little valley seemed more and more like a dream. The dusty land stretched ahead of them.

"My feet hurt, Sam," said Matt. He was walking more slowly.

"Don't think about your feet," said Sam, trying desperately to think of something to talk about so that Matt wouldn't notice how tired he was. "Think about the buffalo. There used to be thousands and thousands of them right here." Matt looked around a little nervously. "Oh, they're gone now," Sam went on. "But I like to think about them. They were kind of like cattle, you know, only big and shaggy.

You remember the buffalo robe Grandpa had for the sleigh? They were furry like that." He talked on and on. After a while he didn't think Matt was listening to his words, just to his voice.

The sun seemed to be sinking faster and faster. Sam tried not to see it out of the corner of his eye. He didn't want to think what they would do out on the prairie in the dark.

Just as he was deciding he would have to think about it, he stumbled over a deep rut in the earth. It was the wagon track. He thought he had never seen anything as wonderful.

"Now we'll be all right," he said.

His voice was so happy that Matt said, "Are we almost home, then?"

"I don't know," Sam had to say. "I don't think it can be too far." But there was no barn and no house in sight. All they could do was go on.

Now the boys didn't talk anymore. They just walked. Matt kept stumbling over the rough track, but Sam didn't dare stop. He put his arm over his small brother's shoulder and guided him along the smoother earth between the ruts.

He was so tired himself that he thought he was dreaming when he heard the sound of horses' hoofs and the creak of a wagon. But he lifted his head.

Driving toward them was the boy who had stood in the doorway of the sod house.

Sam pulled Matt to the edge of the track and waited for the team to go past. He thought of waving to stop the boy, but how could he explain their problem? This boy spoke no English. If only he could ask how far from home they were.

Suddenly he realized that the wagon had stopped. The boy was looking down at him, his dark eyes serious.

They stared at each other. Sam had to say something. In a way he was glad he didn't have to explain that they had almost gotten lost.

He pointed toward the east and said, "Do you know how far it is to our place?" The boy just shrugged and shook his head. But he didn't drive on. Sam waved his arm to the north, trying to indicate distance. He pointed to Matt, drooping beside him.

All at once the boy smiled, a broad joyous smile. He said something and nodded toward the back of the wagon. Sam understood.

"Come on, Matt," he said. "Get in the wagon."

"Is he taking us home?" asked Matt.

"I don't know," said Sam. "But we can't just keep walking."

After they were settled on the floor of the wagon the boy sat for a minute with the reins slack. He looked up the track toward his own house and frowned. Then he shrugged and clucked to the horses. The wagon rocked as the team turned and headed east toward the Ferriers' place. Sam knew what the boy was thinking. He would probably be in trouble for getting back after dark.

Matt was asleep long before they got home. Sam himself had no idea how long the drive took. He roused when the wagon came to a stop.

They were home. Pa and Mama were running across the yard. Pa was lifting Matt out of the wagon. Mama was holding both her hands up to clasp the boy's hands.

"Come in and have some soup," she said. But the boy shook his head, turned the team and drove away. Sam hoped the boy's mother and father would not be angry.

Sam was halfway to the house when Mama caught up with him. "Oh, son," she said in a sharp voice she almost never used. "You are far too late. It's nearly dark." Then she saw the flowers that Sam was still clutching. "Prairie lilies. How beautiful." She went on more gently, "You had better have some soup. Then tell us."

Even Josie was quiet as Sam and Matt ate their soup. Matt fell asleep before his bowl was empty, and Pa carried him to bed. Then he sat down and looked at Sam across the table.

Sam told them about the little valley and about losing their direction.

"There are no landmarks out there," he said. "It's too big. I knew to go south and that's how we found the wagon track. We would have followed it home. But before that I didn't know where we were. I know I shouldn't have got lost with Matt, but I couldn't help it."

Pa and Mama listened until he was finished. Then Pa said, "I think you did well. This country doesn't offer you much help. I've heard of folks wandering in circles, but you had more sense than that. Of course, we can't risk losing you and Matt."

Sam's heart sank. He was sometimes afraid out on that wide land, but he couldn't bear to stay close to the house all the time. He wanted to see the little valley again, if he could find it.

Suddenly Pa grinned. "So we're going to get you young ones some help," he said, and he slapped the table with the palm of his hand. "Yes, sir, the very help you need."

Sam looked at Mama, but she just smiled. He knew it was no use begging his father to say what he was talking about. Pa loved surprises. There was nothing to do but go to bed and wonder.

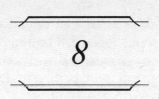

8

THE front steps of the Ferriers' house were built extra wide to make them comfortable for sitting on.

"Someday we'll have a front porch with chairs on it," Pa told Mama, "but there's no reason we shouldn't sit out and enjoy the sunsets in the meantime."

Most evenings after the dishes were done, Mama brought her mending and Pa brought his planning book and they sat on the steps till the sun went down. There was usually enough breeze to keep the mosquitoes away. Sometimes Sam and Josie and Matt sat, too, especially when the sky turned flaming orange and the clouds seemed to be lined with gold. Usually they played tag or King of the Castle.

One August evening Mama said, "James, I think we should lay in our winter provisions soon."

Sam looked out over the dry summer grass. Winter seemed very far away. He could hardly remember snow.

"Some of the women at church were telling me that storms can come early," Mama went on. "We could have snow up to the eaves of our house or a blizzard that lasts for days. Sometimes even the trains can't get through. We're lucky that the corn crop in Iowa was good this year. We have the cash to stock up."

So Mama made a list: ten-pound boxes of dried apples, prunes and raisins, hundred-pound sacks of flour, sugar and oatmeal, canned tomatoes, enough tea and coffee, salt and baking soda to last them through the worst of the winter.

"We'll get potatoes and salt pork when the weather is cooler," she said. "But with these supplies in the cellar I won't have to sit worrying about when the first storm will come."

The day Pa went into Curlew for the supplies he was late getting home. Sam and Josie started the evening chores without him. Sam led the two cows into the barn. Milking was his job. Josie's hands weren't strong enough yet for milking, but she could give the horses their oats. Matt looked after the chickens. He made sure they had water and feed and enough straw in their coop.

The chores were nearly finished when the children heard the gate open and the wagon rattle into the yard. They hurried out of the barn. The wagon was filled with boxes and burlap sacks, and Pa was just climbing down from the seat. But Sam had no eyes for Pa or the wagon.

Tied to the back of the wagon was a horse. A small, stocky white horse with a roman nose.

Pa pushed back his hat and smiled at everyone.

"Hello, Sam," he said. "Hello, Josie. Hello, Matt." He looked from one to the other as they lined up in front of him. "Did you want to hear the news from town?"

Josie stamped her foot. "Oh, Pa. You know we want to know about the new horse."

Sam was peering around Pa.

"He looks kind of small for a plough horse," he said.

Pa turned toward the wagon. "Oh, you noticed Prince," he said in a surprised voice. "Well, I hope you like him because he's your horse. He'll take you all to school. In fact, once he gets a fix on this farm as his home, he can take you anywhere and he'll always bring you back."

Sam wanted to leap into the air and shout, but he knew it was important to be calm around a horse who didn't know you. Josie was already rubbing Prince's nose and Matt was stroking his side, seeing how high up he could reach. Sam stood where he was. He thought that Pa had something more to tell him.

"I wanted a good, trusty horse for you children," Pa was saying. "A lot of folks use an old worn-out workhorse for a school horse. One that can just amble along the path to school with the youngsters on its back and rest all day and bring them home again. But I wanted a horse with more spirit for you, Sam. It's no good for a boy your age to be tied to the house."

Sam couldn't say anything. He could only think of riding toward the horizon, never turning back until he and Prince were ready to head home. He half listened for what he knew Pa would say next.

"Of course," Pa went on, "he's for all of you children and he'll be useful for some work around the place, too."

"Of course," said Sam. He didn't expect to have a horse all to himself. Back in Iowa he had had a pony, but Prince was a real horse and horses had to earn their keep. Anyway, the work he could do with Prince would be more pleasure than chore. He could already imagine riding to town on errands for Mama and bringing cattle in from a far field for Pa.

"Where did you get him?" he asked.

"Chalkey told me about a fellow who was selling out. Didn't take to prairie life. He had some good horses so I went around to see them. Prince is an old-timer and he knows his way around the prairie. I could see that he was sound so I bought him. Go make friends with him, Sam."

It was easy to make friends with Prince. He stood calmly, swishing his tail while all three children petted him and talked to him.

Up close Sam could see that there were grey hairs mixed with the white. Prince was actually a grey horse turning white, as grey horses did when they got older. His mane and tail were white but his eyes were dark, and Sam thought he saw fire in there.

"How old is he, Pa?" asked Sam.

"My guess is he's about ten. The fellow I bought him from didn't know exactly. He got him as part of the deal when he bought his land. He's probably a catch colt, bred out on the range. I'd say he has some quarter-horse in him and some mustang."

Chalkey had told Sam about mustangs. They were horses that had gone wild and lived in herds in the foothills. Now most of the herds were gone because so many settlers had come into that country, but many prairie horses had some mustang blood. Some people didn't like mustang in their horses. It was too unpredictable, they said, and the horses often looked a bit scrubby.

Sam could see that Prince was a bit short in the leg, and he did have a long nose. But already Prince was beautiful to him.

"Horses with mustang blood have good instincts. They are survivors. That's what every creature on the prairies has to be," Pa was saying in a philosophical tone of voice. Then he spoke more briskly. "Sam, you take the first ride. See how you and Prince get along. I'll give you a knee up."

Sam sat on Prince's bare back and looked around. Everything looked different from there: the farmyard small and friendly, the prairie all around as huge as ever but more inviting. Even the horizon did not seem so far away. He leaned forward and stroked Prince's neck, smooth one way, rough the other. He walked the horse around the edge of the farmyard. Then he rode back to where the rest of the family was standing.

"Can I take him just a little way down the wagon road?" he asked. He couldn't stop grinning. "He's a fine horse, Pa. Just fine."

"Go ahead," said Pa. "But don't be long." He raised his eyebrows at Josie and Matt who were bouncing on their toes with eagerness. "There are other riders waiting."

Sam rode out the gate. He turned west. Prince began to trot and then to lope along easily. Sam watched the prairie flow by him and felt the rhythm of the horse's hoofs on the dry earth. After a short time he turned his head to see how far they had come. He was astonished at how small the house looked. He pulled on the reins and sat for a moment patting Prince's warm neck. No longer did he feel like a small creeping thing on a huge table top.

"We may not be big," he said to Prince, "but we can move. Next time we'll go farther." Then he turned his horse and rode back to the waiting family.

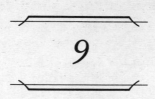

9

THE children spent the next few days getting to know Prince. They showed him his stall in the barn, fed him as much mash as Pa would allow, and curried him until his coat shone and his white mane and tail flowed in the prairie wind.

Sam had ridden many horses on the Iowa farm but none had ever suited him so well as Prince. He could get his arms over the small horse's back and pull himself up. Once up he was at home. From the very first day he felt that he and Prince understood each other.

Josie knew how to ride, too, but she was used to the child-sized pony back on the old farm. The first time she rode Prince alone she spent some time just sitting on his broad back, looking at the ground, before she would let him take a step. He stood quietly until she was ready and then meandered peacefully around the farmyard. It was not long before she was wanting to ride him off down the wagon track.

Matt was fearless but he had a problem. Josie could mount Prince by climbing up on the fence, twisting her fingers in his mane and pulling herself over onto his back. But Matt was too short for that and had to be lifted up. He couldn't mount Prince unless there was a bigger person around to help him.

Then one day he noticed that his feet fit perfectly on the outward bend of Prince's back legs, the hocks. So he grasped Prince's tail, stepped up on his hocks and pulled himself up over the horse's rump.

Pa came out of the house and found his youngest child sitting proudly on Prince's back. When he found out how Matt had got there, he turned a little pale.

"You're lucky that horse didn't kick you to kingdom come," he said. "I knew Prince was a trusty horse for you children. But, Matt, never try that with another horse."

It was Josie who discovered another uncommon way of mounting Prince. She was waiting to go for a ride around the farmyard one day, but Prince was busy taking a long drink at the trough. Josie, as always, was impatient.

"Look," she said to Matt, "I can easily climb on his neck. Then I won't have to lead him over to the fence when he finally stops drinking."

Prince had his nose deep in the trough. He just rolled his eyes when he felt Josie's weight close behind his ears. Suddenly he snorted and lifted his head high in the air. Josie was startled but kept her balance as she slid down the neck onto Prince's back. It was so much fun that she and Matt spent the afternoon waiting for Prince to drink from the trough so that they could slide down his neck again.

When Sam got back from helping Pa haul a wagonload of coal out from town, Josie told him about Prince's new trick. Sam didn't believe her.

"He does it on purpose," she insisted. "He likes to do it. Come on, Prince, let's show him." But Prince was in no mood to cooperate. When Josie urged him over to the trough, he just shook his head and looked the other way.

Sam laughed. "It's true what Mama says. You can lead a horse to water but you cannot make him drink. Come on, Josie. If we go into the barn Prince will forget all about us."

They stood side by side in the hot barn, squinting through a crack in the door, until they saw Prince amble over to the water trough. He didn't object when Josie climbed onto his neck. He even twitched his ears as if he was saying, Just a little farther forward, please.

Then he rolled his eye toward Sam and tossed his head high. Josie slid down onto his back and sat there grinning triumphantly. Sam could almost swear that Prince was grinning, too.

When they told the family about it at dinner, Mama said, "You children mustn't pester that horse. We're lucky to have a horse that likes children so much and you must treat him as a friend, not just something to climb on."

"Your mother is right," Pa said. "You have to treat Prince with respect. He's the one we're trusting to get you children safely to school and back every day."

Sam was a little offended. Surely he could look after the younger ones. But when he thought about it, he knew what Pa meant. Prince would do what instinct told him to do. He wouldn't panic or get confused and he wouldn't need a compass to tell him the way home.

Three times Sam rode Prince to the school and back. Dry runs, Pa called them. "Once Prince knows the way, he'll always get you to school and back. If you have a disagreement with him over which way to go, Sam, you let Prince have his head. Don't argue with him."

Sam knew that Pa was thinking of snowstorms. The clear autumn weather wouldn't last forever.

On the first day of school the three children climbed on Prince. Sam sat in front because Pa and Mama said he was in charge. Josie sat in the middle and Matt was last.

"You're the end rider, Matt," said Pa. "Hang onto your sister. The end rider is in a perilous position." Matt straightened up proudly. Perilous sounded special, even though he wasn't sure what it meant.

Each of the children had a schoolbag. Sam's was slung over one shoulder, but Josie and Matt carried theirs around their necks, bouncing against their bellies. In each bag was a tin box of lunch and a reader brought with them from Iowa. Sam was in the fifth reader and Josie in the third. Matt had Josie's old first reader. They each had a copy book, too, and a pencil.

Mama and Pa had done everything they could to get their children ready for school, but Sam still was not sure he wanted to go. As they jogged along he looked at the expanse of prairie around him and wished he could ride Prince all day instead of being shut up in a little schoolhouse.

But he could feel Josie hanging onto his belt and he knew that he would be heading this direction five mornings a week for months to come.

"Do you know how many pupils will be in the school?" he asked Josie. She paid attention to such things.

"Five from town, I know," she said, "and two others from the country besides us. That's all Mrs. Pratt told me about." Working at the store kept Mrs. Pratt up on all the news, and besides, Mr. Pratt was chairman of the school board.

"Ten," said Sam. "That's not too many." Probably many of them would be little kids like Matt. He wondered whether there was anyone around Curlew his age, besides the boy from the soddy. He wouldn't be at school for sure.

The schoolhouse was exactly like the one the Ferriers had attended back in Iowa, except it wasn't painted yet and it looked more lonesome because there was nothing around it. The Jericho schoolhouse had had some small trees in the schoolyard and a shed for the horses. Mr. Pratt had promised the Curlew school would have a shed before the snow came. In the meantime the horses would have to graze in the fenced schoolyard.

Sam knew exactly what the inside of the schoolhouse would be like. First there would be a cloakroom with hooks for coats—girls on one side, boys on the other. In the big room would be rows of desks with the heating stove and the teacher's desk at the front. As one of the older pupils, he would sit farthest away from the stove.

Nobody knew much about the teacher. Mrs. Pratt said she was from Edmonton and was properly trained. She would be boarding with a family in town. But would she be a stern teacher who used the strap on unruly pupils? Sam wondered about that.

When the Ferriers arrived at the school they saw that there were extra people there for the opening ceremonies. The children were standing in a little group near the steps, but there were several big horses tied to the fence and even two buggies. It was Mr. Pratt who came to the door to call the pupils in.

The school was exactly as Sam had imagined it, but there were grownups standing at the back of the room. The whole school board was there and a few other citizens from the town. Mr. Pratt gave a little speech about what a proud day this was for Curlew and how it meant that Curlew was becoming a town to be reckoned with. He introduced the teacher, Miss Barnett. She looked like a medium person — medium sized, medium aged and neither stern nor smiling. After the speech Mrs. Pratt handed out gingersnaps and oranges to one and all.

After the townspeople were gone, Miss Barnett called the roll and asked each pupil what reader they were in. As Sam had expected, he was the only one in the fifth reader. There was one girl from town in the fourth reader. All the others were Josie and Matt's age.

Miss Barnett looked more lively now. She even looked younger. It occurred to Sam that maybe she didn't like crowds of strangers any more than he did.

She looked straight at Sam now and said, "I'll be counting on you to help with the fires and the horses. I'm afraid I don't know much about horses, and the younger children will need help at the end of the day."

So when school let out, Sam found himself helping a girl and her brother hitch up their little buggy to their stout brown pony. When he was finished he turned to Matt and Josie.

"Now we can go home," he said.

"No, we can't," said Josie. "Prince won't come."

Sam looked across the schoolyard. Prince was standing by the far fence calmly eating grass, but as Sam approached he sidled away just fast enough that Sam couldn't grab his bridle. When Sam moved faster, so did Prince, until he was dancing backwards away from Sam. Sam was sure his horse's black eyes were laughing at him.

Josie was laughing, too, but Matt looked a little worried. "How are we going to catch him, Sam?" he asked.

"He's just bored with waiting all day. He'll give it up soon." Sam hoped he was right. It would be awful if they were late getting home because he couldn't catch Prince.

Just then Miss Barnett came to the schoolhouse door. She was smiling.

"Maybe these will lure him," she said and handed Sam three gingersnaps.

"Thank you, ma'am," said Sam. "Maybe you do know something about horses." He held the cookies out and began talking to Prince. "Come on, you old rascal. You're just having fun with us. Don't you want to get out of this yard?"

Prince stopped backing up and began to edge forward.

"Here, Josie, you hold out these cookies," said Sam. He waited until Prince was almost within arm's reach. Then he stepped forward and caught the bridle. Prince paid no attention. He took the cookies in his soft lips and began to chew. Then he rolled his eyes back at Sam.

Miss Barnett laughed and so did the children. When Sam could stop laughing he spoke sternly to Prince. "Now you have to work," he said.

He lifted Matt onto the horse's back, pulled himself on and then reached a hand down to Josie.

Josie said, "Goodbye, Miss Barnett. Tomorrow we'll bring a treat for Prince." Then they all waved and Sam turned Prince toward home.

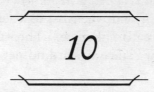

10

SEPTEMBER turned into October. Sam began to look forward to school each day. Three more pupils had shown up and one of them was a boy just a year younger than Sam. He made the schoolyard games much more fun for Sam, but he lived far from the Ferriers. Josie had the same problem with her new best friend, Dorothy.

"You see," Josie explained at dinner one night, "Dorothy lives just as far on the other side of Curlew as we do on this side so we never see each other except at school. Now, if I could just ride Prince over to her house . . ."

"No," said Pa. "Absolutely not. Sam is the only one of you old enough to ride out alone. I hope you understand that, Josie."

"Yes, Pa," said Josie meekly.

In fact none of the pupils saw each other out of school unless they lived in town. But they made up for it by coming to school early to play Red Rover and Kick the Can before the bell rang. During noon hour they played marbles and skipped rope.

Sam liked the games, but his favourite time of the day was the ride to school. The air was cool. Birds rose from the fields and gophers dodged into their holes as Prince passed. Sometimes they met a wagon on the track or saw John or Adam Martingale out working.

One morning Sam heard the sound of a horse coming up behind them. It was overtaking them quite fast and Sam twisted around to see who was in such a hurry.

It was the boy from the sod house. He was riding a big raw-boned black horse.

"Of course he can go faster than we can," Sam said mostly to himself. "His horse has only one rider."

Josie heard him. "And his horse is much bigger," she said. "Prince is kind of small."

Sam was saved from having to answer by a shout from the boy.

"Allo! Allo!"

Josie and Matt answered, "Hello," but Sam, thinking that the boy wanted more room to pass them, guided Prince to the side of the track.

The boy didn't pass. He stopped and smiled shyly at all of them. He was wearing a loose blue shirt and black trousers tucked into the tops of wide boots. On his head was a flat cap with a brim in front that shaded his eyes. He looked tall sitting so high on his horse and Sam thought he might be older than twelve.

After a minute the boy pointed to himself and said, "Gregor."

Josie said in a pleased voice, "It's his name!" She pointed to herself and said, "Josephine." The boy frowned in a puzzled way, so she shrugged. "Oh, call me Josie. Everyone does. Josie."

"Josie," said Gregor.

Then Matt said, "I'm Matthew. But you can call me Matt."

Gregor beamed and said slowly and clearly, "Mat-te-oh."

"It must be the way to say Matthew in his language," said Sam. It was his turn now. "Sam," he said. "Just Sam." Then he realized that Gregor would think his name was Jussam so he said clearly, "Sam."

"Sam," said Gregor and leaned over and held out his hand. Sam stretched out his own hand and they shook. It was the first time he had ever shaken hands with a person his own age, but it felt like the right thing to do.

Gregor smiled the wide smile that turned his eyebrows and all the lines in his face up. Then he said something to his horse and rode off ahead of them. He turned once and waved. They all waved back.

"Where is he going?" asked Matt.

"Pa said his father hired him out to work for someone who is trying to get a house and a barn built in a hurry," said Sam. "I guess his family needs cash. Maybe he can learn some English working, anyway."

"No, he can't," said Josie. "Mrs. Pratt said the people building the house only speak German. We're lucky. At least we can talk to some people who aren't in our family."

As they jogged along, Sam thought that for Josie, having people to talk to was luck. For him luck was not having to work all the time. School was work, in a way, but it was better than spending every day fetching and carrying to build a house you would never live in yourself. He liked doing chores on their own place better. That made sense. And when Prince was included in the job, it hardly even seemed like work.

Prince was turning out to be a reliable horse. That's what Pa said. Except for wanting his after-school treat every day, he wasn't temperamental. He even seemed to have a built-in clock. If school didn't let out exactly at three-thirty, he came and stuck his nose in the open window of the schoolhouse. He didn't look at Miss Barnett, only at Sam. He never made a sound, but his unblinking eyes drew every-one's attention and Miss Barnett would say, "Prince, I think your watch is faster than mine. I'm just about to dismiss them."

When Sam thought about luck, he had to include Miss Barnett. She was a teacher who could laugh, and she never punished pupils with the strap. If one of them was daydreaming or pestering other chil-dren, she said, "Learning is a privilege and if you don't wish to learn you can spend the day in the cloakroom doing nothing at all." Being a bit of day-dreamer, Sam had spent some time there himself, and he had to admit it was boring. Especially because Miss Barnett checked every so often to be sure you weren't just sleeping.

No, school wasn't bad. Still, Sam was always glad when the time came for the ride home. They never hurried; the ride was a break between schoolwork and chores. Prince was happy to jog along at a steady pace. Like a lot of people, Prince preferred not to exert himself.

One afternoon as they neared the Martingale place, Adam came running out of the barn. "Stop, Sam, stop!" he shouted, waving his arms.

"Whoa, Prince," said Sam. He wondered whether to jump down. Maybe the barn was on fire. But Adam ran right over to them.

"I'm sorry to shout at you," he said, "but I'm most worried. The oxen have wandered off. They were in the field for their mid-day grazing and I suppose the gate was left open because they were gone when I came out. You know that we have only one horse and John has ridden off to the south to search. Unfortunately my father and yours have taken a team and gone north to talk to a man who may have some seed wheat. I'm going to borrow Goldie and go to the east. Could you take Prince and go west? I only hope the oxen haven't gone too far. They are wearing their harness. Take some rope so that you can lead them home if you find them."

None of the children had ever heard Adam say more than six words together, but this was a real emergency. Even Matt knew that it was the oxen that made the Martingales' farming possible. To replace them would be very costly, and Sam suspected that for all their books and learned speech, the Martingales were like everyone else out on the prairie, cash poor.

"Of course I'll go," he said. "I just have to stop on the way to take Josie and Matt home and tell Mama where I'm going."

Josie said, "I'm sure they'll turn up, Adam. It would be hard to lose anything that big for very long."

But Sam saw Adam's eyes taking in the vast land all around them. He knew what Adam was thinking. In all that space his oxen could be lost forever.

Mama understood the emergency at once. "Of course you should go and no, Matt, you can't go along. Sam must ride as fast as he can. Just stay near the wagon track, son, and remember that it gets dark earlier now." She gave him bread and butter and a glass of milk and put some dried apples in his pocket. Prince had a good drink of water at the trough and then they were off.

As Sam turned Prince west out of the farm gate, he was suddenly filled with excitement. He hoped he would find the oxen, but not too soon. He had been waiting for a chance to take Prince for a real gallop across the country.

He looked around carefully. There were no oxen to be seen. He decided that he would let Prince gallop for ten minutes or so, then slow him and take a good look around. That way they would cover distance and still take time to search the open landscape.

It took a little urging to get Prince to gallop. He turned his head and looked at Sam as if to say, "Do you really want me to exert myself?" But once they found a rhythm together it was wonderful. Sam felt Prince's warm back rising and falling and the wind blowing his hair straight back. The brown grasses flew past in a blur.

Suddenly he remembered the oxen. "Whoa, Prince," he said. "We have a job to do." He held Prince to a walk for some minutes while he scanned the prairie for the missing beasts. Then he urged his horse to a gallop again. Once Prince had the idea, he willingly galloped, then walked, then galloped. Sam was sure that he was enjoying himself, too.

Looking ahead along the track, Sam thought he recognized the stretch he and Matt had stumbled along in the dusk. He leaned forward to pat Prince's neck.

"I'm glad you're here now, boy," he said.

Then he heard hoofbeats behind him. At first he thought he was just remembering the sound of the wagon on that night. But this sound was too loud for memory. Sam turned around, and there was Gregor on his big black horse.

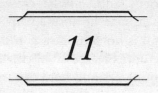

11

THE small white horse and the tall black one stood side by side on the wagon road. The two boys looked at each other.

"Allo," said Gregor. He smiled but he looked puzzled. He pointed down the track and raised his eyebrows at Sam.

"Hello," said Sam. He was thinking hard. If he could make Gregor understand about the strayed oxen, he might be able to help find them.

Sam shaded his eyes and peered all around to show that he was searching for something. Then he pointed at Prince and at Gregor's horse and shook his head. He held up two fingers and hunched his shoulders, hoping he would look a little like an ox.

Gregor looked puzzled.

Sam pointed to himself and to the north side of the track. He drew the shape of a house in the air with his hand. Then he pointed to the south side of the track and drew another house.

"Martingale," he said and looked hopefully at Gregor.

Gregor nodded vigorously. "Martingale," he repeated.

That was good, Sam thought, but not enough.

There was only one thing to do. He slid off Prince's back and got down on his elbows and knees, lowered his head, poked his fingers up above his ears to indicate horns and slowly crawled down the track. After a minute he looked up to see Gregor standing beside his horse nodding and laughing.

Sam stood up. He pointed in all directions, shrugged his shoulders and held out empty hands to show loss. Gregor suddenly looked serious. Sam knew that he finally understood.

Gregor frowned for a moment. Then he said, "Sam!" He put his fingers above his ears like horns and said a word.

Sam said "Oxen? You mean oxen?"

"Oxen," repeated Gregor. They stared at each other. It seemed that a whole world of communication had opened between them.

"Oxen!" they both shouted and shook hands for the second time.

Then Gregor stopped smiling. For a moment he stood perfectly still with his eyebrows drawn together. Then he made a bowl shape with his hands, put his face into the bowl and lapped with his tongue.

"Water?" said Sam.

Gregor spread his arms to show that the bowl was now huge, wider than his arms could reach. He pointed to the southwest. Then he went back to lapping with his tongue.

Sam was very excited. "You mean there's a pond down that way? You think the oxen might be there?"

Gregor picked out the only word he understood. "Oxen," he said firmly and pointed again to the southwest.

Sam scrambled up on Prince. He looked at Gregor. "Will you show me?" he asked, holding his open palm toward the pond. He could now imagine it as clearly as if he had seen it himself.

But Gregor looked uncertain. He pointed along the track to the west and said a word that sounded very much like papa. Sam knew what he was saying. He had to go home now. Sam shrugged and smiled, trying to show Gregor that he didn't mind, though he really did.

Gregor smiled his wide smile. He made a beckoning gesture with his hand. He was saying, Come with me. So Sam followed.

He felt very shy as they rode up to the sod house. Gregor's father was on the roof of a long shed nailing poles in place. Sam thought that he was probably going to cover the poles with sod. Gregor went and spoke to him. The man did not smile at all, but Gregor kept explaining, pointing to Sam and in the direction of the pond.

At last Gregor's father nodded slowly, but Sam saw him look at the sun, which was nearing the horizon. Then he spoke firmly to Gregor. The tone of his voice made Sam think of his own father. Pa might come here looking for him. If only he could leave a message.

When Gregor came over to him, nodding that they could go now, Sam made writing motions in the palm of his hand, pointed to Gregor and to his father, then to himself and to a tall invisible figure beside him.

Gregor made a face and shook his head. He understood, but they had no paper or pen.

Sam thought a minute, got off Prince and took up a sharp stone. He found a smooth patch of dusty earth near the track and scratched out a message. "Pa, Gone to look for oxen. Not far. Sam." He hoped the "not far" part was true.

Gregor looked at the message and nodded. He told his father about it and the man looked at Sam with a small smile of approval. Then he went back to his pounding, and Sam and Gregor guided their horses across the track and started southwest.

As they rode, the tall dry grass brushed their boots and a spray of grasshoppers rose before the horses' hoofs. The slanting late afternoon sunlight made everything golden. The boys couldn't talk to each other, but the sense that someone, a friend, was riding beside him filled Sam with excitement. It was as if they were setting off together on an adventure.

The sky was still blue, but an edge of clouds along the horizon seemed to be rising to meet the sun. They were dark underneath and touched with gold above. Sam was just about to point them out to Gregor when his friend said, "Sam," and pointed ahead of him by lifting his chin. Sam looked. He could see the tops of trees rising above the grass.

In just a few minutes they were riding down a short slope. There in a big hollow in the prairie was a small pond, deep blue like the sky above it. There were reeds all around its edge, showing that in spring the pond would be much bigger. Small willows grew in clumps at the edge of the reeds. And standing knee-deep in the blue water were two large brown oxen.

Sam reached out and slapped Gregor on the back.

"You were right," he said. "The Martingales will be so happy."

Gregor looked pleased but he didn't smile. He was staring at the oxen. Sam looked at the huge beasts again and realized that finding the oxen was just the first step. Now they had to get them out of the pond and home. He had rope wound around his waist, but he could not believe that those oxen would follow him if he tried to lead them out of a place where they seemed so content.

Suddenly he realized that Gregor was off his horse. He was striding through the reeds and into the shallow water. He slapped the oxen on their large rumps and spoke to them in a quiet, firm voice. To Sam's amazement the animals turned toward shore and walked out of the water, sending waves across the pond.

Sam slid down off Prince. He handed the rope to Gregor who quickly tied an end to the harness on each ox. He looked at the long rope with an ox at each end and made a face. Sam had the answer to that problem. He took out his pocket knife and cut the rope in the middle. Now they could get back on their horses and each lead one ox.

When they got to the top of the hill, Sam looked back at the little pond. The water was golden now. It shone in the midst of the darkening prairie. Sam had the feeling that it would disappear as soon as they could no longer see it. He looked around him. The sky was filled with golden clouds that seemed to catch fire in the west near the setting sun.

Gregor laid the reins on his horse's neck and, still holding the end of the rope, he stretched his arms wide as if he wanted to touch the pale gold sky to the east and the blazing orange sky to the west. Then he picked up the reins and moved restlessly on the horse's back. Sam knew what he meant. He wanted to make his horse fly across the darkening land. So did Sam. But instead they walked slowly and steadily, with the oxen plodding behind.

As they neared the track, Sam saw Pa riding toward them. "Good for you, boys," he said. "You've done a good job. The Martingales will certainly think so, too."

"It was really Gregor, Pa," said Sam. "He guessed where the oxen might be and he knew how to get them out of the pond."

"Thank you, Gregor," said Pa. "Thank you from the Martingales."

Gregor looked pleased. He gestured toward Sam as if to say, You deserve some credit, too. But Sam just shook his head.

As they rode along the track, Sam said to Pa, "I guess you found my message."

"I did," said Pa. "Gregor's father made sure I saw it. He seemed to think you were a smart young fellow."

How Pa could know what Gregor's father thought, Sam had no idea. But when they came to Gregor's place, there was his whole family out in the yard to greet them. The dogs barked, the younger children waved and Gregor's mother smiled. Gregor's father came over to Sam and Pa. He put his hand on his chest.

"Ivan Chomyk," he said.

Pa held out his hand. "James Ferrier," he said. "And Sam Ferrier."

Mr. Chomyk put both of his hands around Pa's and shook hard. Then he stepped back toward his family.

Gregor handed Pa the rope he was still holding. He knew that the Ferriers had to be starting home. It was nearly dark and it would be a slow journey with the oxen.

Sam and Pa rode in silence for a few minutes. The wind had blown the clouds away and the stars were starting to show themselves.

Pa looked up and said, "This country grows on you, Sam. I admit it can seem lonely, but it grows on you. I guess you're not so lonely now."

"No," said Sam. Besides his whole family there was Gregor and Prince, especially Prince. Prince was always there, ready to go with him, needing no words. Gregor was a friend, but they did need words. Sam had to figure out what to do about that.

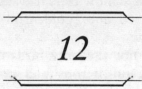

12

EVERY day geese flew over in great V-shaped lines pointing south. Sam felt as if they were pulling winter after them, down from the north. There was a silver edging of frost on the grass in the mornings, and the strong hot winds that had blown all summer were changing into the sharper winds of autumn. People who had been on the prairies for one winter were telling their blizzard stories.

"That wind from the north blows the snow something awful," Mr. Pratt told Pa and Sam. "Why, in a bad blizzard you can lose your way between the house and the barn. Be sure to string up a rope to guide you. At fifty below a fellow will freeze to death pretty fast."

For now, though, the world seemed caught at the end of summer. The sunlight was pale, but it was warm in the afternoons, and goldenrod bloomed in the fields. Every chance he could get, Sam took Prince out for a gallop. He found three more buffalo skulls for his collection and several buffalo wallows. He imagined that fall was a time when the buffalo moved in great herds, thousands of brown shaggy beasts making their way across the dry prairie toward the foothills where they would spend the winter.

One day Sam and Matt rode together out to their valley. The little willow trees had turned yellow, and instead of the red lilies, goldenrod bloomed in the hidden meadow.

Geese were not the only birds that were flying south. Ducks and herons and cranes sometimes seemed to fill the sky. In the evening they flew low looking for water where they could rest for the night.

The duck-hunting season had opened weeks before. Some children brought leftover roast duck to school in their lunch boxes. Pa talked of going duck hunting but he never quite had time and, anyway, he didn't own a shotgun. Sam had gone rabbit hunting with the rifle more than once, and the family had enjoyed several rabbit dinners. Any kind of fresh meat was a real treat, but a duck dinner would be really special.

One day when Pa had gone to town with Josie and Matt, Mr. Corbett stopped by the house. He had taken over the land of the young man who refused to bake biscuits. No one knew just what had become of him, but Sam and Pa were sure that he had gone home to his mother's cooking. Mr. Corbett was reputed to have one hundred head of cattle. He also had several grown sons working with him, but today he was alone.

"I'm running some cattle on the quarter section to the east of Martingales and I'm going out to check on them," he said to Mama and Sam. "Do you mind if I leave my shotgun here? I thought I might get a few ducks, but the gun is in my way." He turned to Sam. "Maybe you'd like to take it and do a little duck hunting yourself. Just remember to fire the left barrel. The right one is jammed. It could give you an awful kick." He leaned the gun against the house, tipped his hat to Mama, mounted his horse and rode off.

Sam looked at the shotgun. John Martingale had talked to him about the sport of hunting water fowl, so Sam knew just what to do.

He looked at Mama. "Can I go?" he asked. "I expect there will be ducks on the pond. I'll take care with Mr. Corbett's shotgun."

"Take care with yourself," said Mama. "Just remember what your father has taught you about guns. I would indeed enjoy a duck dinner."

Sam went to open the gate and Prince trotted right over and nuzzled his neck. He was definitely ready for an excursion. Sam led him out, shut the gate and mounted. The long gun was awkward to hold so he kept Prince to a gentle canter.

Sam knew exactly where the pond was now. He had been there many times, sometimes with Gregor. The two of them had worked out some language between them, but understanding each other took effort. Sometimes it was easier to be alone.

When Sam got to the pond, he was disappointed to see that there were no ducks waiting for him on the still surface of the water. He knew what to do, however. He tied Prince to a willow on one side of the pond. Then he walked around to the other side. He broke off a large bundle of tall reeds and made them into a hiding place like a little tent. John said such a shelter was called a blind.

Sam made himself as comfortable as he could on the hard ground. He peered between the reeds waiting for ducks to land on the pond. He waited a long time. It was warm in the sheltered hollow and the reeds made a pleasant shade. Sam began to feel that duck hunting was mostly boring. The sun on the water was dazzling. He tried squinting up his eyes to rest them.

Suddenly Sam was jolted by a blow to the back of his head. He opened his eyes wide and found himself staring at the sky. Reeds were tickling his face. He must have gone to sleep and fallen backwards.

He was about to sit up when he remembered there might be ducks on the pond. Above all he must not move suddenly and scare them away.

Sam carefully raised himself on one elbow and peered through the tumbled reeds. There were five ducks on the pond. It should be an easy shot, but he didn't dare move enough to get the shotgun in a good position. Slowly he reached for the gun and lifted it. His neck was cricked and the gun wobbled. He had to turn his feet out. He didn't want to shoot a toe off.

Sam was just going to pull the trigger when he remembered about the jammed barrel. It was the left one he had to keep in mind. So he sighted carefully at the nearest duck and fired the right barrel.

The stock of the gun whammed into his shoulder and knocked him backwards. His head bounced against the ground. For several moments he couldn't think at all. Then he heard Mr. Corbett's voice. "Be sure to fire the left barrel. The right one will give you an awful kick." An awful kick for sure, he thought, rubbing the back of his head.

Then he thought of the ducks and sat straight up. There were two ducks floating on the water. The others had flown, of course. But two. With one shot he had gotten two ducks!

Sam collected the ducks and Prince and rode home. The back of his head had a bump on it, but he didn't care. He got into the yard just ahead of Mr. Corbett. Pa, Josie and Matt were already there. For once Sam was glad of an audience. Mr. Corbett laughed when he heard about the kick of the gun, but Pa just kept saying, "Two with one shot. Pretty good, Sam Ferrier, pretty good." Even Josie was impressed.

Mama said, "I'll clean these right away. They're nice and fat. Mr. Corbett, won't you stay to dinner? I'm going to open the last jar of applesauce I brought from Iowa."

Mr. Corbett was pleased to stay. During dinner Sam gave his full attention to the duck and mashed potatoes and applesauce. Mr. Corbett did justice to the meal but he talked, too.

"Did you folks know they get the Edmonton paper in town every Saturday?" he said. "Bring it in on the train, they do."

"I didn't know that," said Pa. "Of course, I don't get to town every Saturday. It will be fine to read the news now and then."

"I have a proposition for you," said Mr. Corbett. "I can send one of my boys into town to get the paper hot off the train every Saturday. Then me and my boys can bring it over for you to read."

"That's mighty nice of you," said Pa. "But wouldn't that be extra trouble? It's out of your way to come here."

"The thing is," said Mr. Corbett, "me and my boys don't read. When my wife was alive she used to read us the paper. Now that she's gone we get hungry for the news and the stories. I was thinking that maybe you'd be willing to read the paper to us."

"Oh," said Pa, and his eyes lit up. "Read the paper out loud! Why, it would be a pleasure."

That is how the Saturday afternoon newspaper readings began. Mr. Corbett and his three sons turned up every Saturday just between chores and supper. The boys were all enormous, bigger than their father, but they did what he told them to do.

"Don't worry about chairs, Mrs. Ferrier," said Mr. Corbett the first time. "The boys will just hunker down."

The three tall young men squatted down and sat on their heels while Pa read the news of politics, crops and the war in Europe. Sam, Josie and Matt sat on the floor and listened, too. Mama and Mr. Corbett occupied chairs. Pa liked to read standing up.

Everybody's favourite part of the paper was the continued story. Every week there was a chapter of a novel full of mystery and adventure. Pa became every character as he read, and all the listeners were spellbound.

If one of the Corbett boys shifted or muttered during the reading, Mr. Corbett, who always placed his chair right behind them, rapped the offender on the head with his bony knuckles.

"You set still and listen to Mr. Ferrier," he would say. "He's doing this for your improvement." Sam was always careful to sit quietly. He was afraid Mr. Corbett would automatically rap anyone who didn't listen the way he thought they should.

One Saturday Pa did go to town, and he wasn't back by the time the Corbetts showed up.

"I'm sorry," said Mama. "James must have gotten held up. He would never want to miss the reading. Wait a bit. He'll probably get here soon."

Mr. Corbett looked around. The little house seemed very full of Corbetts and Ferriers. The Corbett boys looked as though they might bolt into the fresh air at any moment. Sam waited to see what would happen.

Suddenly Mr. Corbett's eyes were resting on him. "Sam Ferrier," he said. "You can read. Stand up and read us the paper."

Sam turned red. He could read, all right, but he hated standing up to read his page in the reader at school. Besides, the newspaper was full of names he couldn't pronounce.

Mr. Corbett would not be put off. "Any young fellow who can shoot two ducks with one shot has enough moxie to read the newspaper to a few neighbours," he said.

Mama nodded. "Yes, Sam. Read to us."

Sam was stuck. He took the newspaper that Mr. Corbett handed him. "I think I'll start with the story," he said in a scratchy voice. Everyone looked pleased.

"You've got the right idea," said Mr. Corbett. "Start with the best part."

So Sam started. At first he stumbled over words, but no one, not even Josie, seemed to mind. As he read, his voice grew stronger. He became interested in what was happening in the story.

About halfway through, the door opened and Pa came in. When he saw what Sam was doing, he pulled a chair away from the table and sat down.

Sam read right to the end. When he stopped, everyone looked at him for a moment. Then Pa began to clap and they all clapped.

"Thank you," said Sam. He was surprised at how easy it had been. But he had done enough. "Will you read the news now, Pa? I think I'd like to sit down."

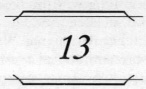

13

SCHOOL ended on the tenth of December. It would open again in early April if the roads were passable. In the winter the weather was too chancey to risk sending children several miles over the bald prairie. They might get caught in a blizzard, lose their way and never get home.

Chalkey told them about a teacher over in Saskatchewan who sent the children home one day when snow began to fall. "But she wasn't really worried," he went on. "She was from back east and she figured western folks were exaggerating about blizzards. She stayed to mark some papers. By the time she decided to go home, she couldn't see six inches in front of her. She ended up spending five days all alone in the schoolhouse, and she had to burn the books to keep warm. I guess she was the one who learned a lesson."

The pupils planned to rush through their lessons during the last week of school so they could spend the afternoons preparing for the Christmas concert. It would be held Friday evening, and every one of them would take part in the program.

On Monday morning, just as Miss Barnett finished taking attendance, there was a great stamping in the cloakroom. In came Mr. Holderman, the agent in charge of the railroad station. He stood just inside the doorway bringing the cold breath of the snowy prairie morning with him. Sam thought he had never smelled such fresh air.

"I hope you'll excuse me, ma'am," Mr. Holderman said. "I've brought you all a little something to help you celebrate Christmas, compliments of the Canadian Pacific Railway." Then he reached back through the door and brought in a little pine tree.

All the children stared. Sam breathed deeply. That was the fresh smell. A pine tree.

It was no wonder the children were staring, he thought. There were no trees at all in Curlew and on the prairies there were only scrub willow trees, drooping toward the pond or wash that allowed them to live. But this tree stood straight, and its stiff branches were thick with dark green needles. It filled the school room with its wild forest scent.

Like the children Miss Barnett was silent for a moment. Then she said, "This will make Christmas very special. The CPR couldn't have done anything nicer for our school."

"They give a Christmas tree to every school along the line," said Mr. Holderman. "It seems that the forests in Canada are just not distributed evenly, so the CPR has to help out."

"Thank you, Mr. Holderman," said Miss Barnett. "Sam, you take the tree."

Sam took hold of the rough trunk. The tree was almost as tall as he was and its branches were straight and even. Sam thought he could never get enough of looking at it. He had seen trees before he came to the prairies — many different kinds. But to see one after all these months gave him a stab of pure joy.

Especially a Christmas tree. The smell took him right back to Christmas on the Iowa farm. Sometimes the Ferriers couldn't get a tree, but Mama always made sure they at least had some evergreen boughs for decoration so that the house would smell like Christmas.

Miss Barnett came and stood beside Sam. "Some of you children have never seen a tree, I think." Several heads nodded. "Well, just as in eastern Alberta we have an abundance of fertile open land, in many parts of Canada there is an abundance of trees. Ten and twenty times the size of this one and thousands of them. Thousands and thousands."

It was hard to look at one small pine tree and think of thousands of thousands of big ones. Miss Barnett rolled down the map and showed the pupils the extent of the forests of the Dominion of Canada, but the children just wanted to look at their tree. Finally Miss Barnett gave up.

"We'll stand our tree in a bucket so that we can keep it watered, and we'll all make decorations for it. I've been saving some silver paper for a special occasion, and this is certainly that."

At the end of the day the tree stood right beside Miss Barnett's desk covered with shining snowflakes and stars. At the top was an angel with a lace skirt and feathery wings made of cut paper and a face painted by Miss Barnett herself.

"Tomorrow I'll bring cranberries to string," said Sarah Martin. She lived in town right behind Pratt's store. "Our tree will be the most beautiful in Alberta."

"Just remember that the tree won't put on the Christmas concert," said Miss Barnett. "You must start practising your pieces tomorrow. But cranberries will be lovely, Sarah."

Sam still hadn't decided what to do in the concert. He thought of offering to be in charge of chairs and coats, but he knew Miss Barnett would not think that was enough. Every pupil was expected to present a piece. Matt was memorizing a poem about Santa Claus. Josie and three of the other girls had made up a play about a little girl who worked at the inn where Jesus was born in the stable. Josie was going to sing "Sweet and Low," a lullaby Pa used to sing when they were babies.

"I don't see why anyone in Bethlehem would sing about the wind of the western sea," said Sam to Josie as they rode to school the next morning.

"Pa sings about it," said Josie, "and he has never seen the western sea, either. It just happens to be my favourite song. Anyway, you don't even know what you're going to do for the concert."

But the Christmas tree had given Sam an idea. There was a story in one of their books at home called "The Fir Tree." It was by Hans Christian Andersen.

On Tuesday Sam brought the book to school. He showed the story to Miss Barnett.

"Could I read this at the concert?" he asked.

"That's a fine idea, Sam. But you'll have to shorten it."

Sam didn't mind. He didn't like the end, anyway, because the tree got thrown on a trash heap and regretted ever being a Christmas tree. Sam doubted that trees had regrets, but he liked the part of the story where the tree was in the woods wanting to be a Christmas tree. That didn't sound too likely, either, but he thought folks would like it, especially with a tree right there to look at.

It was really Mr. Corbett who gave Sam the feeling he could read to a whole school full of people. He still talked about how well Sam had read the story from the paper. Sometimes now he asked that Sam take a turn reading the newspaper on a Saturday. Sam almost looked forward to those times, but when he thought about four tall men waiting for him to read because they couldn't, he felt strange.

"Why can't they read, Pa?" he asked one Saturday after the Corbetts had filed out of their kitchen. "They're smart, I know that."

"They're smart enough," said Pa. "But folks who don't learn to read when they're young usually don't think of doing it later. I expect the Corbetts have spent their lives working all the time. They just never had a chance to go to school."

"Like Gregor," thought Sam. Gregor would get a chance to learn English someday, he guessed. But maybe by then it would be too late for reading to come easily to him.

On Tuesday, Wednesday and Thursday Sam read "The Fir Tree" over and over to himself. Pa listened to him read it aloud each evening after supper. "Loud and clear, son," he said. "You want every listener to hear every golden word."

On Friday morning before school began, Sam spoke to Miss Barnett about a new idea he had.

"I have a friend who doesn't know English," he explained. "He can't come to school because his family can't spare him from the farm, but I thought that in the winter when there isn't so much to do I could teach him to say some words and read them. But I need a book."

"Is it the Chomyk boy?" asked Miss Barnett. "It would be wonderful if he could learn English. I know Mr. and Mrs. Chomyk want the best for their children, but there's no one who can talk to them about school. They really are alone in a new country. I think you have a very good idea, and I have just the book to start you off." She went to her desk, took out a big book and handed it to Sam. It was full of pictures of animals and plants and houses and people. Every picture had a word beside it.

"This is perfect," said Sam. "Thank you, Miss Barnett. I'll bring it back in April."

On Friday afternoon Miss Barnett dismissed the children early so that they would have time to get home and have supper before returning to the school for the concert. Sam carried his book home so he could take a last look at the story after supper, but he barely had time to open it.

He and Matt both had to put on clean white shirts and neckties. Josie was very pleased with her red dress with lace ruffles down the front. Her only complaint was that she had to look at herself in sections in Mama's small mirror.

When they were all dressed, Mama lined them up to check their faces and give their hair a final brush. Then they all piled into the wagon.

It wasn't until they were halfway to the school that Sam realized the book was at home lying on the table.

"We have to go back, Pa. We have to," he said desperately.

"You know there isn't time for that," Pa said firmly.

Mama turned around to look at Sam. "You know that story so well you hardly have to look at the book when you read it to us," she said in an encouraging voice. "You can just say it in your own words."

"I've heard it so often I could take your place," said Josie.

Sam felt sick. Pa was right. They couldn't go back and it was his own fault anyway. He held on to a faint hope that Miss Barnett would let him off. "I can't read the story when I don't have the book," he would explain. But it was a very faint hope.

When they got to the school the whole family waited while Pa and Sam put up the horses in the newly built shed. The children all wanted to see Mama and Pa's faces when they saw the Christmas tree. They had agreed to save it for a surprise.

As they came into the cloakroom, it seemed to Sam that they must be earlier than he thought because there was no sound of chattering from the schoolroom. Yet they had to hunt to find hooks for their coats.

Maybe we're late, he thought. Maybe Miss Barnett is waiting just for us.

The family gathered at the door and Pa opened it quietly as if he, too, thought they might be late. But it was not the program that was hushing the crowded room. It was the Christmas tree.

The tree had been beautiful when the children went home at the end of the school day. Now it was magical. On each branch was a burning candle. The light shone and glittered on the silver snowflakes and stars. The chains of cranberries glowed like rubies. And the little tree stood straight and proud, bringing the wonder of creation into the bare school room.

Mama and Pa found places on the benches around the room. Matt, Josie and Sam squeezed in behind the desks with the other children. Still more people came in.

When at last all were seated, Miss Barnett walked to the front of the room and said, "Welcome to the Curlew School Christmas concert. Since we are so lucky as to have a real Christmas tree and since the candles will not last for the entire program, I think we should start with a story about a Christmas tree. Sam Ferrier will begin with a reading of 'The Fir Tree' by Hans Christian Andersen."

Sam's legs wouldn't move. His face felt stiff with fear. Josie was right next to him. She leaned closer and whispered, "I dare you to do it, Sam. I dare you." He turned to look at her and she smiled. He noticed that her smile, unlike her words, was a lot like Mama's. He stood up.

Standing by the tree gave him some courage. Surely people would be looking at the tree, not at him.

He cleared his throat. "I decided to tell you the story in my own words. I hope you like it." The dimly lit room seemed to be full of faces, all staring at him. He paused and the silence got longer and longer. Then Josie's face caught his eye. She frowned at him and her lips silently shaped the words, Go on!

Sam took a deep breath and began. "There was once a pretty little fir tree that grew in a forest."

Then, in his mind, he could see that little tree growing among taller ones, and the story unfolded easily.
He hardly saw the faces in front of him now. When
he got to the part where the tree was a Christmas
tree, he made it happier than the story in the book
did. He thought that a tree like the one next to him
would be happy to be shining with candles and silver
stars, if it had feelings.

"And the children and the tree were happy
together that Christmas day," he ended. It seemed
that the ending had come very quickly. Suddenly his
knees began to shake.

Miss Barnett stood up. "Thank you, Sam," she
said. "I've never liked that story so much. Now let
us all sing 'Deck the Halls.'"

Sam sat in a daze through the rest of the program.
He was surprised at what he had done. He heard
Josie sing her song in a sweet voice. With a big grey
shawl covering her red dress, she really managed to
look like a humble maidservant. Matt made everyone laugh, which made him very happy.

They all agreed that the Christmas concert was a
great success. At the end Mr. Pratt distributed little
bags of nuts and beautiful hard candies in wavy rib-
bon shapes.

Miss Barnett came up to Sam and said, "It was a
good idea to tell the story, Sam. What made you
think of it?"

Pa answered for him. "It's necessity that often
leads to the greatest deeds, wouldn't you say, Miss
Barnett?"

Miss Barnett smiled at Sam. "It does if the person
is truly prepared and you certainly were. Merry
Christmas to all of you."

On the way home in the wagon Pa said, "That was a fine way to end your first term at Curlew School. Now we'll just hole up for the winter. We're pretty lucky. We have plenty of food, and the house is tight. We just have to think of ways to keep busy."

"I have something I want to do," said Sam. "I want to teach Gregor English. I guess he can ride over sometimes or I can go over to his place. Prince will be needing exercise."

"That's a good idea, son," said Pa. "Rabbit and Lady will be needing exercise, too."

Sam wondered why Pa would expect him to take Rabbit or Lady. They were the work horses, not often used for riding. They pulled a wagon or a plough well, but for riding they were stodgy.

Anyway, Prince was practically Sam's. Why should he ride any other horse?

14

THE next day Sam worked with Pa to get the barn ready for the winter. Pa covered cracks between the boards with tarpaper while Sam gave the stalls an extra good cleaning.

He was just starting to pitch in fresh bedding straw when Pa said, "You'll only need to take care of two of the horse stalls, Sam. You see, we have a problem."

He laid his hammer on a low beam and turned toward Sam. "We can't afford to feed all the horses all winter. We don't have the money to buy oats, and anyway, we don't have enough hay for five horses. It's a problem lots of folks out here have, but they have a solution."

Sam stood with the pitchfork in his hand and stared at Pa. Was he going to sell Prince?

Pa went on, "People turn the horses loose on the prairie to fend for themselves for the winter. The horses run in herds. They can find grass under the snow to eat and folks build shelters of fencing and straw to make wind breaks for them. They get along all right."

"But you won't put out all the horses," Sam managed to say.

"No, we have to have a couple. We'll need to get into town and there may be some work we can do around the place. I've decided to keep Rabbit and Lady in the barn. They have never faced a prairie winter. The other three have. Why, Prince was probably born out on the range."

"But Prince is small and he's used to being almost a pet," said Sam. He couldn't believe that Pa would turn Prince out.

"The horses look after each other," said Pa. "They choose a leader who keeps them together and finds shelter when they need it. Prince is a tough horse. He'll be fine."

Sam went back to pitching straw. He could hardly see where it was landing because of the tears in his eyes.

Josie was furious when Pa told the rest of the family about the horses.

"Prince will die," she said. "He's used to people who share their lunch with him. The horses will fight and he'll get killed or he'll starve. I know he will."

Matt just said, "I'll miss him, I'll miss him."

"I'm sorry," said Pa, "but facts are facts. We can't afford to feed five horses. Rabbit and Lady are a good team of work horses. We can't run a farm without a team like that. I could sell Prince and Goldie and Pete. But this way they'll be back next summer."

Sam sat feeling miserable. He knew what Pa was saying. If they had to lose a horse it would be better to lose Prince than a good plough horse. There was no use arguing about it.

All that night Sam dreamed about blizzards. He was searching for Prince in the swirling snow. Again and again he saw a shape in the blinding whiteness,

but each time he got near, it disappeared. He woke up exhausted.

At breakfast Pa said, "Ride out with me, son, to set the horses loose. You'll see that they accept it. I'm sure it's happened to all three of them before."

So Sam got Prince from the barn. Pa rode on Rabbit leading Pete and Goldie. Rabbit would bring both Pa and Sam back. As they left the farmyard, Sam could see Matt and Josie standing at the front window. He knew they were crying.

They rode about five miles to the north. Pa said that a number of settlers had agreed to set their horses loose in the same area so they could form a herd.

After that they didn't talk much. Sam was feeling Prince's muscles move beneath his hide and watching his mane blow in the cold wind. He wished he could tell him that this was not his idea.

The place they stopped was no different from any other part of the prairie except there was a U-shaped structure built of posts and wire with straw heaped inside it. Pa said it was a shelter. Sam didn't believe that loose straw would even cut the icy wind, but he couldn't say anything.

He slid off Prince's back and went around to his head. He held out a piece of biscuit he had saved from breakfast. It had apple butter on it. Prince took it with his soft mouth and munched it. Sam rubbed his long nose.

"Take care of yourself, boy," he whispered. "I'll be waiting for you."

Pa reached a hand down so that Sam could swing up behind him. Then he turned Rabbit and urged him to a gallop. Sam looked back. Pete and Goldie were already nosing the snow, hunting for grass. But Prince was gazing after Sam and Pa. He followed them with his black eyes until Sam couldn't see him anymore.

The next morning Josie got up from the breakfast table and began to clear the dishes away. Suddenly she stepped over to the window.

"Look," she said. "I knew Prince wasn't a range horse."

They all looked. Prince was standing at the farm gate. Pa got up.

"You children stay here," he said. "I'll take him out alone this time."

But before he left he went into the bedroom and they heard him pull the storage box from under the bed. When he came through the kitchen he was carrying the rifle. Josie gasped and Matt's eyes were big and round.

Sam took two steps toward the door, but Pa held up his hand.

"I'm not going to shoot anything," he said. "But I have to drive Prince away or he'll keep coming back. A shot in the air will do it, I hope."

He pulled on his boots and his heavy jacket and went out with the gun in the crook of his arm.

The children sat glumly around the table. Mama cleared away the dishes, poured hot water from the kettle into the dishpan and began to wash the bowls. She didn't ask anyone to dry. Sam thought of the cold empty land where Prince would have to live through the coldest emptiest months. He hated the prairie. He hated it for Prince and for himself. Without Prince the prairie seemed like a prison.

Once the dishes were done, Mama must have thought that they had brooded long enough.

"It's just two weeks to Christmas," she said. "I'm counting on you children to decorate the house."

They would not have a Christmas tree or evergreen branches, of course, but Mama had been saving paper. Some was coloured and some was white.

— "Paper chains will make the house look festive," she said. Josie and Matt cheered up immediately. Josie mixed up some flour-and-water paste and Matt began cutting sheets of paper into strips.

"Pa left me some work to do," said Sam, and he went out to the barn where he spent the morning fiercely nailing strips of tarpaper over every tiny crack in the walls. By the time Pa came back he was hot and the job was nearly done.

Pa looked around and said, "Good work, Sam. Stop pounding a minute. Prince will be all right. He trotted off in the direction of some other horses. He's not alone."

Sam said, "Yes, Pa," and went back into the house. There he was swept up in preparations for Christmas whether he liked it or not.

That's the way it was every day. If he didn't want to make paper chains or cut snowflakes from the pages Matt had torn out of his old scribbler, he had to go out to the barn where Prince's empty stall made him feel sad and angry.

Jabbing the pitchfork into the stacked-up hay and tossing it hard into the stall helped some. At least Rabbit and Lady didn't try to cheer him up. Sam thought they missed the other horses. And they probably hated staying in the barn as much as he hated staying at the house.

He was so gloomy for the first few days after Prince was gone that Mama finally said, "Sam, the only help for you is work." She gave him a little blank notebook and set him to planning the crops they might plant next year and the yield they might expect. "Who knows what will come to pass," she said, "but if you draw the plans neatly and do the calculations properly, it may help your Pa."

Pa looked at Sam's figures about the yield of wheat and barley they might expect if the weather was perfect, "If we're that lucky we'll buy a Model T Ford," he said. "What do you think about that, Sam?"

A Model T! It was the first interesting thing Sam had thought about since the school concert. A few people in Curlew had automobiles. It was wonderful to watch them wheeling down the street all by themselves. But there were hardly any roads that wouldn't shake a car to bits or get it stuck in the mud depending on the season. A horse, now, could go almost anywhere. And there he was, thinking about Prince again.

Mama saw his face change. "Sam," she said, "it does no good to mope. Prince will either survive the winter or he won't. He's lived his whole life on these prairies. I think he has a good chance."

Sam didn't know why, but Mama's blunt words made him feel better. He still worried, but he stopped moping and began to think about Christmas. The next time Pa drove Rabbit and Lady to town, Sam went along.

He took the few dollars he had earned helping Adam build a fence and went into Pratt's store. There he picked out a photograph album for Mama and Pa. Pa took pictures sometimes but they were all jumbled loose in a box. He knew Mama would like sorting through them and sticking them on the handsome black pages of the album. He looked at hair ribbons for Josie but in the end he got her a wooden top. She would like it better. He really wanted to get a jack-knife for Matt, but they cost too much so he settled for a bag of marbles. He didn't see why they couldn't play marbles in the house or in the barn instead of waiting for spring.

So Sam was ready for Christmas in spite of everything. The house was strung with paper chains and hung with snowflakes, and a frozen turkey, ordered from Edmonton through Mr. Pratt, was thawing in the coolest corner of the house. Sam went to sleep on Christmas Eve with the happy feeling that Christmas, at least, could be counted upon.

He was right. The only thing missing was the smell of the Christmas tree. The biggest surprise was a sleigh. Pa called it a cutter, and as soon as there was enough snow they would all go for a ride.

But Sam liked Pa's present even better than the cutter. It came in a thin flat package. Sam felt it carefully through the paper. "It feels like a picture."

Pa looked mysterious. "Ah, but what picture? That is the question." Sam tore open the package.

It was a picture of Sam standing by the house holding up the two ducks he had shot. Looking over his shoulder was Prince.

Sam was amazed. He had forgotten that Pa had taken a picture that day. Looking at it he remembered how Prince had waited patiently for him while he waited for the ducks. Then they had come home together, triumphantly.

"Where are you going to put it, Sam?" asked Pa after Sam had thanked him several times.

Sam looked around. "Not in the bedroom," he said. "It's too cold in there. Could I put it right here beside the window? Then we can all see it whenever we want to."

"Good," said Pa, and he got a hammer and drove in a nail. Sam hung the picture and they all looked at it and thought of Prince.

"He's fine," said Mama. "I'm sure of it. Look what a smart horse he is."

Sam looked at the picture for one more moment. Prince was smart. He just hoped he was lucky, too, out there on the prairie. He turned away from the picture.

"That turkey sure smells good," he said.

15

ONCE Christmas was past, winter settled over the prairie as if it never intended to leave. The days were very short. The Ferriers got up in darkness and went to bed in darkness. When the sun shone it was pale, as if its fire was cold. Mama had to light the kerosene lamp about four o'clock if anyone wanted to read.

There was just enough snow on the ground to keep the runners of the cutter gliding smoothly. It wasn't the heavy soft snow Sam remembered from Iowa. This snow was grainy and dry like sugar, and it flew up from the horses' hoofs as they trotted over the frozen ground.

"The whole world is frozen," Sam said to Matt one morning when he came in from doing chores. The earth felt as hard as iron, and metal was too cold to touch. The leather harness had to be brought into the house and warmed by the stove before it would bend easily.

But worse than the cold was the wind. It never stopped blowing. At night Sam lay in bed listening to it drive tiny icy grains of snow against the house. In the morning he half expected to see holes worn through the walls as if a giant piece of sandpaper had rubbed against them all night.

But the little house he had helped Pa build stood firm and, as Pa said, it was tight. They didn't wake up with snow on the floor, though the air in the bedrooms felt like ice water when Sam and Matt cautiously slid out from under their quilts in the morning.

They grabbed their clothes and dashed for the kitchen where the big stove made a pool of warmth. Everyone took turns dressing in that warmth. By breakfast time the pool reached to the table, so that their oatmeal stayed warm while they ate it. Pa had made sure they had plenty of coal. The lean-to was stacked with it. As the wind howled and the house shivered, Sam thought how strange it was that a shed full of black dusty chunks made them feel safe.

The short days seemed crowded with work that had to be done. Mama set lessons for each of the children to do each day. On baking day the table was taken up by bowls and rising loaves, and somehow they all ended up kneading and shaping the dough.

Baking was fun but laundry was terrible. The wet wash had to be hung near the stove or it would never dry. If there was a bright day Mama washed even though it was not wash day. Sam and Josie hung the clothes to dry outside. It seemed to Sam that they froze instantly, but somehow the wind dried them anyway.

Sam often thought about Gregor. The book Miss Barnett had lent him sat on the shelf with the books Pa read aloud in the evenings. It reminded Sam of his plan to teach Gregor some English. The problem was, how could they get started when they never saw each other?

Sometimes, when the weather was not threatening, Sam went into Curlew to get the mail. He usually took the cutter. Neither Rabbit nor Lady was a pleasure to ride. Lady simply did not like to be ridden. She poked along or went into a bouncing trot that was very uncomfortable. Rabbit was reliable but slow. When Sam rode Prince he felt that they were working together. Riding Rabbit was like riding a table.

But the cutter was fun. Rabbit dashed along the wagon track and the cutter blades sent a whirl of snow up into the air. Sam always hoped he would meet Gregor on the track, but he never did. And if they did meet, how would he manage to invite Gregor to come home with him and learn English?

One day Sam was out in the farmyard breaking the ice on the water trough so that the cows could have a drink. He heard the sound of the gate and looked up from his work.

There was Gregor, riding into the yard.

"Sam," he called out.

"Gregor!" said Sam. He motioned toward the house. "Come in."

Gregor shook his head. He reached into his pocket and pulled out a letter. He held it out to Sam but Sam grinned and wouldn't take it.

"No," he said. "Come into the house. We all want to see you."

Gregor nodded and put the letter away. He climbed down from his horse and handed the reins to Sam.

"Oh, yes," said Sam. "I'll put him in the barn. It's too cold for him to stand."

When the two boys got into the house, Sam pulled out a chair and pointed to it. Before Gregor sat down he took out the letter and handed it to Mama.

"It's from Iowa," she exclaimed. "Oh, thank you, Gregor. We haven't had a letter from home since Christmas." She sat down to read it.

Sam looked at Gregor. He didn't know how long Gregor would stay, and he didn't want to waste any time.

"Matt," he said, "I want to show Gregor a picture in your reader. Could you get it for me?"

He opened the book to a page that showed two boys sitting at a table reading a book together.

"Look, Gregor," he said. "This is you, Gregor, and this is me, Sam."

Gregor nodded but he looked a little confused.

Sam pointed to the book in the picture. "English," he said. "Gregor, Sam, English."

Gregor studied the picture. Then he looked up at Sam and smiled broadly. "English!" he exclaimed.

"Yes, English," said Sam. He went to the shelf and got the book Miss Barnett had lent him. "Look," he said, "I'll teach you some of these words."

They turned the pages. There were pictures of birds and animals and plants, but now Sam realized that most of them lived in far parts of the world. What was the use of teaching Gregor to say penguin and llama and redwood trees? Those words wouldn't help him talk to people around Curlew, Alberta.

"We need pictures of ordinary things," he said to Mama, who was reading her letter for the third time.

"This book is interesting but I don't think it will help Gregor at all."

"I know just what you need," said Mama. "Eaton's catalogue." She went to the bedroom and brought out a thick paper book. "I put it away because we really can't buy anything till some money comes in, but it will make a splendid school book."

Sam opened the catalogue to a whole page of hats. He pointed to a broad-brimmed one.

"That's a hat, Gregor," he said. "Hat."

"Hat," said Gregor. He had a little trouble with the h-sound, so he repeated it a few times.

Sam had an idea. He got his hat and put it on his head. "My hat," he said. Then he got Gregor's hat. "Your hat."

Gregor pointed to his hat and said, "Your hat."

"No," said Sam. He thought for a minute. "Matt, come and help me." With the help of Matt and Matt's hat, Gregor soon had the idea of mine and yours as well as hat. Then Sam turned the pages of the catalogue again and stopped at shoes.

At the end of an hour Gregor could say, "Give me my hat and shoes," and "Where are my hat and shoes?" Sam felt very proud.

Gregor looked out the window. The light was fading. "Where are my hat and shoes?" he said and pointed west.

"Go home?" said Sam.

Gregor nodded. He put on his jacket as well as his hat and boots and grinned his wide grin. "Hat and shoes and Gregor go home," he said and opened the door.

Sam watched him ride away on the black horse. He felt a little envious, but he knew the Chomyks had only two horses. They had no choice but to feed both of them through the winter.

After that Gregor came often for an English lesson. They used the catalogue for words and made sentences that Sam decided would be useful. Matt and Josie helped by acting things out and by talking to Gregor just the way they would talk to anyone. Sam thought Gregor learned most by just talking.

Mama suggested that Sam teach him to read the words they found in the catalogue as well as to say them. Once he started reading, Gregor wanted to write, too, so they all got busy helping him. It was fun because Gregor learned so quickly.

Once Sam said, "Should I come to your place sometimes? You always have to ride over here."

"No, thank you, Sam," said Gregor. "So small a house, so many people."

Sam understood. It was probably dark, too. But soddies were warm, he had heard.

"Could you teach your little brothers and sisters English?" Josie asked another time.

"Later," said Gregor. "Now I will help earn money. Later there will be time for English and school. Not yet."

So Sam knew that Gregor would not be going to school when it started again in April.

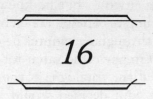

16

FEBRUARY began with a five-day storm. The ordinary rush of the wind changed to a howl that started as a low moan, rose to a high screech and sank again to a moan but never stopped. The wind carried snow with it until the bedroom windows were nearly covered. Then it changed its mind and angrily blew the great heap of snow clean away.

In those five days the sun was lost. Daytime was faintly grey and nighttime was black dark. Mama kept the lamp burning all day. Every morning Sam watched her tilt the kerosene can to see how much was left in it.

Once she saw him looking and said, "Don't worry, Sam. There's enough here for more days than this storm is likely to last. Anyway, we have candles. And there's plenty of coal. That's the most important thing."

Sam knew she was right, but he felt that the circle of yellow light around the lamp helped hold the storm outside the thin walls of their house. All day long they sat around the table with the lamp in the middle, reading or sewing or playing dominoes. Sam always sat with his back to the stove. From there he could look up and see the white shape of Prince in the photograph beside the window. The horse almost seemed to be in the lamplit circle with the family.

Pa had strung a rope to the barn just as he had been advised to do many months before. On the first day of the storm he said to Sam, "I'll do the morning chores, but I'd like your help in the afternoon."

Sam spent the day close to the stove. He played games with Josie and Matt and mended some harness. Pa was teaching him how to make holes with the awl and draw the waxed thread through. The day passed slowly. By chore time he was glad to put on his jacket and boots. The circle of lamplight seemed more like a prison than a haven.

Pa eased the door open just far enough for Sam to slip out, but even so the cold blast of wind filled the little house. Sam got a good grip on the rope. Then Pa came out behind him and pulled the door shut firmly.

Once Sam was away from the shelter of the house, it seemed that there was nothing in the world but wind and icy snow. He knew Pa was behind him, but he could not see him if he looked back or hear him if he shouted. It was fifty steps to the barn. By the time Sam got the barn door open, his face was numb and his fingers were stiff inside his heavy mitts.

Once they got inside, Sam and Pa stood for a minute getting their breath. The still air and the warm smell of the animals made the barn seem less cold than it was.

"It's a good thing we covered up every crack," said Pa. "And it's a good thing we have five animals in here, plus the chickens, of course. They keep each other warm."

Sam thought for just a moment of the horses out in the storm. Were they huddled together to keep from freezing? Then he got on with the milking.

The cows weren't giving much milk these days and he wasn't sure they could get the little bit there was safely to the house, but the animals still had to be milked.

When all the chores were done, Sam and Pa wrapped themselves up again. Pa put the lid on the milk pail and they went back into the storm. By the time they made it to the kitchen, Sam was grateful to be back in the circle of lamplight.

That night and every night of the storm, the howling came into Sam's dreams. He saw Prince trying to outrun the bitter wind, running from wolves, always running. He woke in the mornings as tired as if he had been running all night himself.

By the fourth day of the storm, everyone in the family came to breakfast with heavy eyes. Pa looked at the plateful of biscuit Mama put on the table and said, "It's been days since we've had bread, Clara."

"Exactly how do you expect me to make bread?" said Mama crossly. "I have to keep the stove hot so that we won't freeze, but a foot from the stove it's too cold for bread to rise. We're lucky to have biscuit."

Everyone stared at Mama. Pa looked a little ashamed. Suddenly Matt said, "I know. You can put the bread in Josie's bed. It's the warmest place in the house. It's not fair but it is."

"How could you put bread in my bed," said Josie scornfully.

"I could, you know," said Mama. "If I had it ready, all wrapped up in towels and put it in your bed as soon as you got up, I think it would be warm enough to rise. Matt, thank you. This wind has paralyzed my brain and my manners."

On the fifth morning of the storm Mama did exactly as she had planned. By noon the bread was baking and they ate it straight from the oven, spread with apple butter. Matt got all the end crusts, his favourite part.

On the sixth morning Sam woke up with a strange feeling. Something was missing. He lay in bed listening.

It was the wind. The moaning and shrieking were gone. The storm had blown itself out. Frost covered the windows, but the light that glowed through it was pale pink.

Pa was already in the barn. "I'll help him, Mama," said Sam. "I'll eat breakfast later."

He put on his coat, hat, boots and mitts and stepped out the door. The world was quiet, and the sun was rising red in the east.

By the time the chores were done the sky was pale blue. Sam ran from the barn to the house. The air was so cold he could feel it burning as he gulped it down his throat. In spite of that he felt like running straight out onto the prairie. But he went into the house instead. He needed hot oatmeal inside him before he did any such thing.

Pa was already sitting at the table. "I'm going to take the cutter and go into town, Sam. Want to come?"

It was tempting to think of town and people to see and talk to, but Sam's legs wanted to run, not ride in a cutter. He looked away from Pa and saw

Josie's face, shining and eager. "Take Josie, Pa. I'd rather go for a walk."

Everyone stared at him. "Take a walk in this terrible cold?" said Mama. "Don't you think it's too dangerous, James?"

Pa considered. Then he said, "You've been cooped up all this time, Sam. No wonder you need to run. If you use your common sense you should be all right. That means wrap up well and don't go out of sight of the house. If you see even one single cloud, head for home. This weather won't last and a storm can come up fast. I'm told there is usually a lull of at least a day or two between storms, but you can't be sure."

"What about you, James?" said Mama.

"Josie and I will use common sense, too. We won't linger, will we, Josie? And if we see a cloud we'll head for home. Even if snow starts, Rabbit and Lady know the way."

"What about me?" said Matt. "Can I go with Sam?"

Sam's heart sank. Just for an hour he wanted to be alone. Just for half an hour.

"No, Matt," said Mama. "I need you with me. We'll play some games."

"Outside games," said Matt firmly.

"Of course," said Mama. "I'm tired of this house, too, but, unlike Sam, I'd rather not be alone. We'll play Fox and Geese."

After breakfast they cleared the table in double-quick time. "You three run along," said Mama. "I'll do these up later. We don't want to waste the sun."

They all put on their warmest clothes. Sam had two thick sweaters and he wore them both, as well as three pairs of socks. He turned the flap of his cap down over his ears and even tied the strings under his chin, something he ordinarily scorned to do. Then Mama wound his scarf around him so that it covered his mouth and nose.

"Now remember what your father said," she reminded him a little anxiously. His mouth was so muffled up that he could only nod in reply, but he nodded hard. He had no intention of freezing to death on the prairie.

He decided to walk straight north. That direction the land rose a little and he could see the house from farther off. That was what he told himself, but really it was because Prince had been set loose to the north, and that made his feet want to walk that direction. Of course, there was no telling where the horses were now. Prince could be fifty miles away. Or more.

Sam started to feel gloomy thinking of Prince so far away, but then the glory of the sun shining on the snow and the great sense of space around him wiped everything out of his mind except the wish to run. So he ran. The earth under his boots was as hard as bare rock, and the snow was thin and dry.

When he could run no more he suddenly remembered his promise to Pa and he turned around. The house was still well in view, though small in the distance. The scarf over his mouth was damp with his breath. He tried to shift it to a dry spot with his clumsy mittened hand. Then he turned around slowly.

As on the very first day when he walked out on the prairie, he was in the middle of a great tilting circle with an arching blue sky overhead. But now the blue of the sky was cold and pale and the tops of the taller golden prairie grasses showed above the gleaming white snow. He was in the centre of a blue, white and gold world. He began to run again, partly from exhilaration and partly from the need to keep warm.

Suddenly he heard a great rumbling sound. Thunder. He stopped. Fear made his bones feel weak. Thunder in such cold weather must mean a storm coming fast.

Sam looked up at the sky. The high blue was clear. No clouds. But the thunder rolled on.

Then Sam realized he was hearing the thunder partly through his feet. The frozen ground was shaking. He turned around again slowly, squinting against the dazzle of the sun on the snow.

He saw horses galloping toward him. A whole herd of them running fast, their manes and tails flying in the frosty air.

Sam could not move. Maybe the horses would gallop over him, but he could not move.

He could see their colours now, black and brown and spotted. One that must be Goldie, a dark one that was surely Pete. But where was Prince? There must be a white horse among the others. He scanned the moving mass of bodies anxiously.

Then he saw that the herd had an order to it. That black horse was always in the rear and at the front was a white horse, like a shadow against the white snow. A white horse galloping straight toward him.

As the herd came closer Sam kept his eyes on that white horse. Surely he was smaller than the others. Surely it was Prince.

It was. Prince was galloping straight toward him.

But when the horses were so close that Sam could see Prince's black eyes looking at him, the whole herd suddenly veered away. All the horses followed Prince and he led them in a great circle around Sam. Three times they circled. Then Prince tossed his head and neighed. All the other horses neighed, too, and Prince led them away, straight away from Sam toward the north.

Sam watched them until they were out of sight. Once again he was alone in the middle of that great expanse of white and gold under the arching sky. He stood until a tingle in his right big toe told him he had stood long enough. Then suddenly he was running again, running toward home.

It was a long run. Sam was surprised at how far he had gone. He reached the farmyard just as Pa was leading Lady and Rabbit into the barn. They had been to town and back while he was out on the prairie.

Sam rushed panting into the barn. It was a few minutes before he could speak. Pa stood waiting. Finally Sam took a deep, steadying breath.

"Pa," he said. "Pa, Prince is the king of the horses!" And he told Pa all that had happened.

When he was finished, Pa held up both hands as if he was going to say something very important.

"Sam," he said, "if Prince is the king of the horses, we'll have to change his name."

"Change his name?"

"Yes, Sam Ferrier. From now on the horse once known as Prince will be called King."

For a long moment Sam thought about it.

"King," he said to himself, and then out loud. "King. It sounds right to me, Pa. It sounds true."

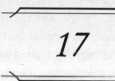

17

S AM told the story of how he had seen Prince being king of the horses many times. The family wanted to hear it over and over. Mr. Corbett and the boys declared it was better than anything in the newspaper. Gregor simply beamed and said, "Yes, King. I know this word. King. A good name."

Josie talked to Sam privately one day when they were doing chores. "Will Prince know King is his name when we call him that? Will he mind being just a pet when he's been a king all winter? Maybe he won't want to come back, Sam."

Sam automatically kept on milking. All winter he had worried that his horse would die on the winter prairie. Now Josie had come out with a new worry that he had pushed to the back of his mind. The horse he had seen leading a whole herd was King, not Prince. Maybe he had gone wild.

"You could ask Pa," he said slowly. "Maybe he knows what happens with the horses at the end of winter."

"Sam, you know Pa will say that King will come back. But what do you think? You know King best."

"He was glad to see me. I'm sure of that," Sam said. "But he's like a wild horse now. Free. We can get him back all right, but I don't know whether he'll be so friendly again. He's the king of the horses now and I'm glad. He's King but I hope he's still Prince, too. We'll see when spring comes."

But spring was very slow in coming. Everyone looked for signs. The days got longer. The storms only lasted two or three days, and little by little the cold lost some of its edge.

The children played outside every day unless there was a storm. The snow was soft enough now to make a good snowball or a sturdy snowman.

And they played Fox and Geese. First they trampled a huge circle in the snow. Then they made paths like spokes leading to the centre. One player was the fox. The others were the geese who had to flee from the fox along the paths. Around and around they ran.

It was most fun when Gregor played, too. Of course, he came over to learn English, but Sam said that if they talked while they played, it could count as a lesson. So Josie, the fox, would scream at Gregor, a goose, "I'm coming to eat you! I'm going to catch you with my sharp teeth."

"No! No!" Gregor would shout back. "I'm running fast. Never will you catch me!" Sometimes he laughed so hard that he fell over and got caught.

When they were out of breath and cold, they went into the house for hot sugary tea and cinnamon buns.

Gregor could tell them now about his family and how they came to Alberta. "My father and mother waited a long time to come. They saved their money. They sold everything. Then we waited more for travel papers. When they came some of our ticket money had gone for food. My uncle who was with us, he gave us his money and did not come."

"Where is he now?" asked Mama.

"Still in Ukraine." Gregor looked sad. "But again we save our money. We will send it to him and he will come. Someday. Now we make our farm, our new home."

"Like us," said Josie.

Yes, Sam thought, like us but harder.

The end of March was near but winter still wasn't ready to leave. "I can't wait to go back to school and see some people," said Josie. "School will start soon, won't it?"

Pa went into town and talked to Mr. Pratt. He came back with good news. "School will begin on the first Monday in April," he said.

"How will we get there?" asked Sam. He hoped Pa would say they would have to bring King home.

"You'll take Rabbit and go in the cutter as long as there is snow on the ground," said Pa. He looked at Sam's disappointed face. "About the time the snow goes, the horses should come home. If they don't, we'll go and get them. That's a promise, Sam."

Sam felt strange going back to school without Gregor, after they had sat together over books for so many hours. Gregor could read Josie's reader now with some help. It seemed wrong that he couldn't take his place at a desk with the rest of them. But Gregor's uncle was waiting for ticket money, and Gregor had to help earn it.

"I'll ask Miss Barnett if we could borrow a reader for you," Sam told Gregor. "Then you could keep up a little. Anyway, you can talk to anyone now when you get the chance."

"I like that I can talk," said Gregor. "I thank you, Sam."

"It was the best part of the winter," said Sam. He was embarrassed. "No thanks necessary."

Even Easter on April 23rd didn't seem like spring. The day was clear, so the Ferriers could go to church in the cutter, but with snow stretching to the horizon it was hard to think of flowers and new life.

When they got home, Mama looked at the table set for Easter dinner and said, "I can't help missing flowers. Even one little crocus would make it seem like Easter."

Still, there was ham and cranberry jelly that Mama had carefully saved all through the winter.

They were just going to sit down when there was a knock at the door. It was Gregor. In his hand he held a small package wrapped in white cloth.

"An Easter gift," he said. "For you, Mrs. Ferrier, from my mother. She made." He handed Mama the package and she carefully unwound the wrapping.

"It feels like an egg," she said.

One egg? They all wondered.

She set the package gently on her plate and turned back the last layer of cloth.

"It is an egg," she said. "The most beautiful Easter egg I have ever seen."

They all crowded close to look. The egg was covered with a beautiful fine pattern in red and black and yellow.

"It's a work of art," said Pa at last.

"Your mother made it?" said Josie. "How could she make such a pattern on an egg? How does she do it?"

"I cannot say," said Gregor. "My mother always does this with wax and colours. In Ukraine she made many. Here more difficult. She can't find many colours. Still, it is beautiful."

"Yes, it is," said Mama. "Look." She got a teacup and set it upside down in the middle of the table. Gently she put the egg in the little hollow in the bottom of the cup. "There," she said. "Instead of flowers, a beautiful egg. Thank you, Gregor. You have brought Easter to our table." She paused a moment to admire the egg. "Would you stay and eat with us?"

"No, I thank you but I must go home. But my mother she says thank you that you teach me English and to read. She is very glad."

Then he was gone. The Ferriers sat down to eat their dinner and to marvel at that egg. "It's something to keep forever," said Mama, and they all agreed.

The next morning Sam bundled himself up to go out to the barn. He opened the door and stood still on the doorstep for so long that Mama said, "What is it, Sam? Is there something in the yard?"

"No," said Sam. "It's the wind. Feel it, Mama."

Mama, Josie and Matt all came to the door. They stood with Sam, just feeling the soft wind that was blowing from the south. Sam took off his hat and felt the wind stir his hair.

"This wind smells good," said Matt.

It did. There was a whiff of earth and grass in that gentle wind.

"Well," said Mama. "I think the wind is telling us winter is over. Sam, you'll all be late to school if you don't get out to the barn. Josie, you run and help him."

As they walked, the snow seemed to be wilting under their feet, flattening out and sinking.

Pa was already in the barn, pouring water into the chickens' pan. "I don't think we should take the cutter today, Pa," Sam told him. "The snow may be gone by this afternoon."

"You're right, Sam. You'll have to ride Rabbit. He won't like it any more than you will, but we have no choice."

"We need King," said Josie. "Our King."

Sam got busy currying Lady, but it wasn't her solid brown shape he saw. He saw a white horse galloping at the head of a whole herd of horses, his black eyes shining, his mane blowing. King of the horses.

"We need Pete and Goldie, too," said Pa. "If they don't all come back in a day or two we'll have to go get them. You two skedaddle back in and eat your breakfasts. I'll finish up here."

Now Sam looked for King every day. He could imagine him at the farm gate in the morning or the evening, hoping for oats. As he rode Rabbit to school and home again, Sam's eyes searched the prairie for the band of horses. But there was no sign of them.

At dinner on Friday Pa said, "I need Rabbit here on the farm. I just can't spare him any longer."

"We have to get King back," said Josie. "But how will you find him, Pa?"

"That shouldn't be a problem," said Pa. "Corbett tells me that the band of horses has been sighted just a few miles northwest of here. We'll go out tomorrow, Sam, and bring in our three."

Sam woke up very early the next morning. He tiptoed to the kitchen to look out the window. There wasn't even a hint of light in the east. The house was cold but Sam was too excited to go back to bed. He got dressed and went out to the barn to get King's stall ready for him. He put some straw in Pete and Goldie's stalls, too, but he gave King extra.

He got back into the house just as Mama was shaking down the ashes in the stove and adding more coal.

"This is an important day, isn't it, Sam?" she said.

"It sure is." He wanted to tell Mama about how worried he was that King wouldn't want to come home, but Matt came in to get dressed by the stove, and Josie was clamouring for her turn.

Pa and Sam started out right after breakfast. They both rode Rabbit, just as they had when they came home after setting the horses loose so many months before. Sam hoped he would ride home on King. Pa seemed to have no doubts about that.

"King may be a bit wild after a winter in the open, Sam. It may take him a few days to settle down with us. Don't be too disappointed if he doesn't seem glad to see you."

Sam resolved that he would only be disappointed if King didn't come home with them at all.

As they rode they constantly scanned the horizon for horses. It seemed to Sam that they had ridden a very long way. The sun was bright and he was afraid that its dazzle would keep him from seeing the horses if they were far away.

Then suddenly, to the west where he had seen nothing just a moment before, Sam saw dark moving shapes. He reached around Pa to point.

"Look! There they are."

And there they were. Twenty or thirty horses grazing. As Sam and Pa got closer, they saw that most of them were bunched together, but three or four were scattered around at a distance from the herd. Sam couldn't see King, but he thought he could spot Pete.

"We'll move toward them very slowly," said Pa. "I'm hoping King or one of the others will recognize us and remember oats and come to us." He kept Rabbit at a slow, even walk. None of the grazing horses seemed to notice their approach except the nearest one, a spotted horse not much bigger than a pony. It lifted its head and moved uneasily.

When they were close enough that Sam could see its shifting eyes, the horse suddenly neighed loudly and bolted toward the main herd. All the horses lifted their heads.

Then out from the centre of the herd came a white horse. He didn't look in the direction of Sam and Pa. He just ran away from them toward the northwest with all the other horses behind him.

There was nothing Pa and Sam could do. They just sat and watched their horses and two dozen more disappear into the distance.

"By golly," said Pa, "he's set sentries. Did you see those horses grazing away from the others? King set them on watch duty to warn the herd of approaching danger. We're going to have to outsmart him. But how?"

Sam didn't have the answer. They rode home in silence. Sam wanted King back more than anything, but he couldn't help thinking, "What a smart horse. He really is a king."

On Sunday Adam Martingale went with them. Pa carried sacks of oats and Adam had a lasso. He knew how to use it, too, which surprised Pa and Sam.

"I've been practising in the barn over the winter," said Adam. "I'll give you lessons, Sam. If you people are going to run any cattle, it's a necessary skill."

Once again they found the herd grazing peacefully with the sentry horses placed far enough away to give warning. "I guess we'll have to start with them," said Pa. "As long as they do their job we don't have a chance with the main herd."

He opened a sack of oats, slid off Lady's back and quietly approached the nearest sentry horse with the bag open in his hands. The horse raised its head and sniffed. It looked toward the herd but it remembered the smell of oats and was drawn to Pa.

"Sam," said Pa quietly. "Begin talking and ride closer to the herd. Talk to King. Maybe he'll recognize your voice."

So, while Pa enticed the spotted sentry horse with oats, Sam rode toward the herd.

"Hey, boy," he said. "Hey, Prince, we've changed your name. You're a king now and we call you King. Come on, boy. I've missed you." He talked and talked, getting closer and closer to the bunched-up horses. He could see Pete now and Goldie and a flash of white in the middle of all the horses.

Suddenly the black sentry horse to the west of Pa gave a resounding neigh. The group of horses parted, and Sam could see King. For a moment King looked at him. He wheeled and rose on his hind legs. He seemed to survey his herd. Then with a long neigh he broke out of the cluster and headed toward the north, away from Pa, Sam and Adam. Away from home.

The three of them rode slowly back.

"We'll have to have a round-up," said Pa. "We need more men and horses for that. Tomorrow I'll ride out and talk with some of the others who have horses in that herd. We should be able to get them in on Tuesday or Wednesday."

Sam had no doubt that these men would bring the horses in. Look what a few frontiersmen had done to the buffalo. But he hated the idea that King wouldn't want to come home. What if he was a friend only because he had to be?

18

ON Monday Pa rode off on Rabbit to organize people to bring the horses in.

"You children will just have to miss a day of school," he said. "It's a pity but I don't see any help for it."

Mama did not seem sorry that they would all be home for the day. She had a gleam in her eye.

"This is our chance to do a big washing," she said. "All winter I've just kept us decent but not properly clean. I'm going to wash all the quilts as well as the sheets and clothes. There's a good drying wind blowing. I'll need all of you to help."

Sam pumped pail after pail of water and lugged it up to the house. Matt grated the bar soap and dissolved it in warm water. Josie stood on a chair and stirred the washing in the big wash boiler while it heated on the stove. Mama used a stick to lift the wet clothes from the steaming water into the washtub. Then she and Sam took turns scrubbing them on the washboard.

They put the smaller things through the hand-cranked wringer, but the quilts were too thick to go through so the two of them had to twist the heavy fabric between them.

Clotheslines full of wet laundry stretched from the house to the barn by lunch time. Sheets and tow-

els, quilts and pillowcases, shirts and dresses all
flapped in the brisk spring wind.

Mama looked at the sky. "Most things will dry
by dark," she said. "The quilts can stay out over-
night if necessary. It's not going to rain tonight."

They had bread and cheese and canned tomatoes
for lunch. They didn't expect Pa home till later, so
they just sat down and ate. They all felt that they
had done a good morning's work.

Sam was just going to ask Matt if he wanted to
walk up to the little valley when he heard the sound
of the gate.

"That must be Pa," he said. Then he heard it
again. "No, it's somebody having trouble with the
latch. I'll see who it is." He jumped up and opened
the door.

Beyond the bright rows of laundry he could see
the farm gate. And at the gate stood King. He was
reaching his head over the gate and pushing with his
chest to make the latch rattle.

Pa has brought King home, thought Sam. He
looked beyond King and there were Goldie and
Pete. No Pa.

Sam felt swamped with joy. He wanted to shout
but his voice was stuck in his throat.

King, however, was not speechless. He lifted his
head and whinnied. Then he pushed against the gate
again.

"Look, everyone," said Sam finally. "King has
decided to come home."

They all came to the door. "Don't rush out," said
Sam. "Pa said to take it easy. They might act kind of
wild. But we can welcome them. Mama, is there any
apple butter left?"

Mama spread bread thickly with apple butter. Sam took a piece and walked slowly down to the gate. He was going to take it very easy. He would not be disappointed if King wasn't friendly right away.

But King was leaning farther over the gate, reaching out with his lips, ready to nuzzle up the treat Sam was holding.

Sam laughed. "Oh, King," he said. "I'm glad you're back. Do you mind being King? It's your new name."

King pushed against the gate again and looked straight at him.

"I guess it's all right with you," said Sam.

Goldie and Pete came over wanting a treat, too, and Josie and Matt were ready with more bread and apple butter. Mama came to rub the noses of all the horses.

"It does seem right to have them back," she said. "We'll let them in but we'll have to tie them to the fence until the laundry is dry. You children can bring them some oats. They must be hungry."

Josie and Matt brought oats in pails and Sam got the curry comb. King looked a bit thin, but he was still sturdy. His coat was thick and rough, almost shaggy. A coat for a prairie winter. Sam worked for a long time combing out the tangles and burrs.

Mama came out to check the laundry. "I wonder why he came home now," she said.

"I think he saw the laundry," said Matt. "It's like flags. Maybe it reminded him of us."

"I think he got to remembering home after he saw Sam and Pa," said Josie. "What do you think, Sam?"

Sam looked at King standing there so calmly. He remembered this horse racing across the prairie leading the herd with his mane flying.

"I think he wanted to come home when he decided to come. He didn't want to be brought. Did you, King?"

King nickered a little and nuzzled Sam's shoulder.

"He seems to like his new name," said Josie. "It's kind of funny how easy it was to change to King."

"That's because it's the right name," said Sam. "Mama, could I go for a ride?"

Mama hesitated. Then she smiled. "Yes," she said. "But don't go far. Remember, King has to get used to our ways again."

Sam knew she, too, was thinking of a wild horse galloping across the prairie. But King seemed perfectly happy to canter gently along. As they went west along the wagon track, Sam thought of all the places they could go. All the places they would go. The pond, the buffalo wallow, the little valley, Gregor's house. And town. And school. Maybe he would find more buffalo skulls or something even better. There was no telling.

Sam looked at the blue sky and at the newly green prairie grass. Suddenly he saw that the grass was so thick with tiny purple flowers that it seemed to reflect the sky.

"Oh, King," said Sam. "If we rode straight on maybe the earth would just melt into the sky."

But instead of heading for the sky, Sam and King turned around and headed home.